the knot
bridesmaid
HANDBOOK

the knot
bridesmaid
HANDBOOK

Help the Bride Shine
Without Losing Your Mind

CARLEY RONEY and the editors of TheKnot.com

CLARKSON POTTER/PUBLISHERS
NEW YORK

Copyright © 2009 by The Knot, Inc.

All rights reserved.
Published in the United States by Clarkson Potter/Publishers, an imprint of the Crown
Publishing Group, a division of Random House, Inc., New York.
www.crownpublishing.com
www.clarksonpotter.com

CLARKSON POTTER is a trademark and POTTER with colophon is a registered
trademark of Random House, Inc.

Some material included in this work originally appeared on the website
www.TheKnot.com.

Library of Congress Cataloging-in-Publication Data is available upon request.
ISBN 978-0-307-46204-6
Printed in the U.S.A.
Design by Jennifer K. Beal Davis
Illustrations by Mary Lynn Blasutta
10 9 8 7 6 5 4 3 2 1
First Edition

The Bridesmaid's Bill of Rights

HERE ARE YOUR OWN LAWS TO LIVE BY . . .

✦ You have the right to freedom of speech—sort of: If asked by the bride whether you like something, you may respond honestly. If not asked, you must forever hold your peace.

✦ You have the power to act with the bride's best interests in mind. If a troubling situation arises, you have the authority to direct the photographer, bounce rowdy guests, or ask the DJ to cease playing "Macarena."

✦ You have the right to weigh in on your dress. You also have the right to hope with all your heart that the bride chooses one that you find less than terrifying. However, in the event your dream does not come true, you have no right to complain for a single second.

✦ You have the right to veto cruel and unusual underwear: a Wonderbra that gives you porn-star cleavage, Spanx that cut off your circulation, panty hose the color of a bad sunburn.

✦ You shall not be forced by the bride to permanently alter your appearance for the sake of looking good in the wedding pictures. This includes, but is not limited to, dyeing your hair, removing tattoos, or getting a nose job.

✦ You have the right to call it quits on assemble-four-hundred-DIY-favors duty, but only after putting in enough hours to make your glue-gun hand hurt. Don't forget, the bride needs your help (and she also considers these things "fun").

✦ You have the right to keep your other job, your other friends, and, yes, your other interests while undergoing your tour of duty. While your loving bride may occasionally forget this important fact, you will remind her *nicely*.

✦ You are relieved from your duties after the bride and groom head out on the honeymoon. If you want to do more, you can. But technically, you're free at last!

Bride X

Bridesmaid X

contents

INTRODUCTION

8

CHAPTER ONE

The Ground Rules

10

CHAPTER TWO

Play Nice

28

CHAPTER THREE

Get Your Wallet Ready

46

CHAPTER FOUR

You'll Love the Dress

56

CHAPTER FIVE

Shower Time

72

CHAPTER SIX

Bachelorette, etc.

100

CHAPTER SEVEN

This Is It: The Wedding

116

CONCLUSION

Lessons Learned

142

ACKNOWLEDGMENTS

143

INDEX

144

introduction

Congrats! Your friend or family member has just popped the question: "Will you be my bridesmaid?" You smile and gush, "Of course! I'm so happy for you!" Then it clicks. "Oh my gosh! What do I have to do? What will I have to wear? What will it *cost* me?"

We've all heard bridesmaid horror stories. You know the ones: scary dresses in pastel colors, maxed-out credit cards, crazy bride breakdowns. The truth is, being a bridesmaid has gotten kind of a bad rap. And sometimes its reputation is not that far off the mark. Some brides go overboard (we have even been a little guilty of it ourselves). We also know many bridesmaids (no, of course not *you*) who act pretty badly, too. So consider this book a referee that brings both sides, the bridesmaid and the bride, together. You can use this to defend yourself and to remind yourself that you've actually agreed to these duties.

So what exactly *will* you need to do? You'll need to make the bride look good on the biggest day of her life, assist her with details, and help her stay sane. There is no task too big (using your graphic design degree and two full days of work to "make her wedding web page prettier"), too small (hot-gluing quarter-inch ribbon around tiny little baskets for her favors), or too embarrassing (pretending to be her because she doesn't dare to make the call to break up with her calligrapher) for you to handle. You've gotten a great start already: You're thinking things through, you're organized, and hey, you've got this book. So dive right in and get started!

CHAPTER ONE
the ground rules

so you think all you'll have to do is parade down the aisle in the perfect shade of pink? Here are the three big roles you'll play as one of the bridesmaids. (By the way, if you're the maid of honor, expect a few more responsibilities; more on that on page 18.) You'll be a therapist-on-call. When the bride needs to vent, gets cold feet, or just can't sleep at 2 a.m., you're one of her appointed confidantes, someone she can count on to listen without judgment and assure her, "Everything will be okay." You'll be the social director, too. It's up to you to be cheerful (you can fake it if you must), impeccably organized, and able to get everyone on the dance floor in a conga line in record time. And, of course, you'll be the personal assistant. Happily dropping Friday night plans to stuff envelopes just comes with the job description.

The Real Deal on What You'll Do

We know, weddings are a whirlwind of activities, events, and arrangements—and that's not just for the bride and groom. Granted, you won't have to carry around an eight-pound accordion file full of tear sheets, stationery samples, and ribbons, and you probably won't have half the local florists, cake bakers, and photographers on speed dial. But you will have your own list of to-dos—and that list includes more than just "show up on time." Some tasks you can anticipate, organize, and plan; others might pop up at the last minute, or even seem particularly strange or stressful. The key is to be both prepared *and* flexible. That way, if something arises that requires your attention as an attendant, you'll be on top of it.

What to Expect: A Bridesmaid's Top 10 Jobs

These jobs are all fair game. Don't wait for the bride to ask for your help—go ahead and offer it on any one of these. We rated them based on Bridesmaid Do-Gooder Points: Rack up fifteen or more shoes and you truly deserve the Maid's Medal. Okay, we know, we know, you're not *really* keeping score anyway.

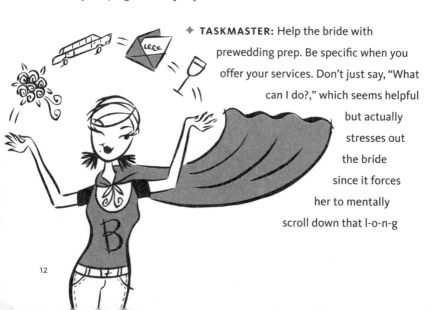

✦ **TASKMASTER:** Help the bride with prewedding prep. Be specific when you offer your services. Don't just say, "What can I do?," which seems helpful but actually stresses out the bride since it forces her to mentally scroll down that l-o-n-g to-do list. Instead, "Would you like me to help you shop for bridesmaid dresses/stuff invitations/pack for the honeymoon?" is a good start. Not sure what to offer? Think about where you might want some help if you were in her shoes.

SCORE: ◢

✦ **PERSONAL SHOPPER:** Scout out bridesmaid outfits. This actually helps you, too. If you find a cute silver cocktail dress *before* she finds that bright orange ruffled thing, well, you get the picture.

SCORE: ◢ (THIS ONE IS REALLY FOR YOUR BENEFIT!)

✦ **EVENT PLANNER EXTRAORDINAIRE:** Help to plan, cohost, and pay for the shower and bachelorette party with your fellow bridesmaids. Don't just go along for the ride—or, worse, make the planning process difficult for everyone else. Leave the bride out of most of the details. More on this in Hot Topic on page 21.

SCORE: ◢ ◢ ◢

✦ **LIFE OF THE PARTY:** Sounds tough, right? Well, just showing up on time to all the prewedding events, including the engagement party, wedding rehearsal, and rehearsal dinner, won't cut it. You also should be warm, welcoming, and enthusiastic. Don't worry; it's totally normal for your face to hurt from smiling so much.

SCORE: ◢ ◢

✦ **ERRAND GIRL:** On the day of the wedding, you'll be on hand to confirm flower delivery times, meet and greet the ceremony officiant, even satisfy wedding party junk-food cravings.

SCORE: ◢ ◢ ◢ ◢ ◢

✦ **MORNING PERSON:** Show up for the wedding as early as the bride asks (even if it's an evening affair and she wants you to report to her home at 9 a.m.). You'll be dressed, made up, and on time for prewedding portraits. You may also be on decorating duty at the ceremony site or in charge of helping the rest of the bridal party get ready (especially if you're a whiz with a curling iron or eyeliner).

SCORE: 👠 👠 👠 👠

✦ **HOSTESS WITH THE MOSTEST:** Step up as auxiliary hostess at the reception by introducing guests, making sure they know where the bar is located, and inviting them to sign the guest book. Also, stand in the receiving line (even if your feet are killing you!) at the bride's request, and woo all wallflowers out onto the dance floor. Don't worry, we'll cover what you're supposed to do and say in the receiving line once we get to chapter 7.

SCORE: 👠 👠

✦ **MASTER OF CEREMONIES:** Participate in all the wedding traditions and revelry. Even if the groomsman you're paired with has bad breath and two left feet, you will walk down the aisle and waltz with him without a grumble. If you're single, you'll cheerfully stand up to catch the bridal bouquet. No idea how to do the hora? Wing it. You're required to be a part of all the family fun.

SCORE: 👠 👠

✦ **HANDLER:** Look out for the bride in general. If she needs help getting ready, be there. If she's gotta go during the reception, haul her bustle to the bathroom. Make sure she's stunning at all times: Tell her if her nose is shiny, a hair is out of place, basil is stuck to her front tooth, or there's lipstick on her cheek.

SCORE: 👠 👠 👠

✦ **GIFT GURU:** Yes, even though you're spending tons of cash on everything else, like travel, the dress, and the parties, you do still have to buy shower and wedding presents. Consider going in with one or a few of the other bridesmaids. It'll give you more buying power, and two heads are better than one when it comes to gift ideas. Sometimes the entire bridal party pitches in for one knock-her-socks-off gift, like a helicopter ride on her honeymoon. More on gifts and parties in chapter 3.

SCORE:

i got creative

"I've been a bridesmaid at six weddings, and I've had to handle some pretty strange assignments for my friends. But the weirdest by far was my college roommate's. She's obsessed with *The Phantom of the Opera,* so she wanted *Phantom* masks at every table at the reception. I ordered them online from a costume store, but two days before the wedding, they still hadn't arrived. Turns out they were back-ordered! So I wound up papier-mâchéing ten of them in my apartment!" —lesmis86

Now that you know what goes into being a bridesmaid, you may have jitters about the job. Better not let the bride in on that—it won't exactly jibe with that rule about helping her stay sane. Trust us, she doesn't have time to calm your nerves—she has a few things to think about herself, like, hello, totally changing her life forever. As far as she's concerned, you need to play it cool, calm, and collected.

If you're really worried, and, gulp, even wondering if you might be able to get out of this, you *can,* but you better have a darn good excuse (see Ask Carley on page 21). Remember, though: This is supposed to be fun— something you'll look back on and be so glad you did. Besides, she asked you because she not only cherishes you in her life, but also because she thinks you can handle the job.

Top 10 Excusable Excuses

There are some reasons you can give when declining an invitation to be a bridesmaid that might float. Note: A five-star rating is definitely a good excuse!

1. "I'm pregnant and my due date is the day of the wedding."
   RATING: ★ ★ ★ ★ ★

2. "My sister/brother is getting married the same day."
   RATING: ★ ★ ★ ★ ★

3. "I'm getting married myself just the week before . . . and I have a lot on my mind at the moment, not to mention I'd have to cut my honeymoon short."
   RATING: ★ ★ ★ ★

4. "I'm completely broke and there's no way I could afford to participate."
   RATING: ★ ★ ★

5. "I've just been promoted . . . to a job in another country."
   RATING: ★ ★ ★ ★

6. "I broke my leg and my crutches won't fit under the chuppah."
   RATING: ★ ★

7. "I was once engaged to the groom . . . so it's a bit of a conflict of interest, don't you think?"
   RATING: ★ ★ ★ ★ ★

8. "I'm flattered, but we haven't spoken since grade school. Maybe you'd rather give this honor to someone else."
   RATING: ★ ★ ★

9. "Oh no, that's the same date as the bar exam."
   RATING: ★ ★ ★

10. "I think you're making a big mistake."
    RATING: ★ ★ ★ (Note: This one *will* get you out of the wedding, but don't plan on speaking to the bride again.)

Top 10 Inexcusable Excuses

Do yourself and the bride a favor and don't even try these. Trust us, they won't go over well.

1. "I'm allergic to wedding cake."
2. "I can't leave my dog alone at night."
3. "I saw *27 Dresses* and it freaked me out."
4. "I really wanted to lose fifteen pounds before donning spaghetti straps."
5. "If I'm your bridesmaid this time, all our friends will want me to be in their weddings, too . . ."
6. "I'm insanely jealous."
7. "I'll overshadow you."
8. "I don't really have the time."
9. "It depends—will you give me some sort of present?"
10. "My cousin's husband's friend asked me to be her bridesmaid, and her wedding is the same day."

Seriously, if you can't be in the wedding, don't wait until the last minute to break the news. Tell the bride up front, as soon as possible, so she can find another taker. If you agreed initially but something came up, be honest. When you turn her down, make sure to express your gratitude as well as regrets and ask if there's anything else you can do on the wedding day. Maybe you can still be in her wedding party in a lesser role. Be prepared for her to be angry/hurt/shocked/panicked by your response, but allow some time for things to blow over. If you have a *really* good reason for turning her down, she's bound to understand.

The Ultimate Honor: Maid or Matron of Honor, That Is

If you've been given this esteemed position, you're the one the bride is counting on the most; the MOH is a VIP. You can expect more responsibility than the other girls, and the rest of the attendants will likely seek out your approval as the bride's right-hand woman (in other words, the one who can most easily get through to her right now). You'll have all of the same duties as the rest of the bridesmaids, but you'll also play these four big roles.

You'll be the bride's advocate. You are closest to the bride and you keep her best interests in mind. You step in and negotiate with her mother or wedding planner when she is being pushed in a direction you sense she doesn't like. You support her—always.

You'll be her fashion stylist. You'll help the bride shop for her gown and accessories, and you'll make sure the rest of the bridal party is dressed the way she wants. Of course, if she asks you, "What do you think of chartreuse strapless?" it's okay to exert your fashion rights and express reluctance. She did ask, after all. You don't actually get veto power here, however. If she still wants to go with chartreuse, you've got to get on board. (More on how to sell the dress on eBay later.)

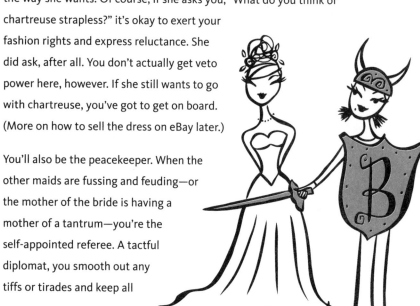

You'll also be the peacekeeper. When the other maids are fussing and feuding—or the mother of the bride is having a mother of a tantrum—you're the self-appointed referee. A tactful diplomat, you smooth out any tiffs or tirades and keep all those negative vibes far away from the bride.

And, finally, you'll be the communications coordinator. You'll make sure to keep everyone who needs to be in the loop informed of the whos, whats, wheres, whens, and how muches.

What to Expect: A Maid of Honor's Top 10 Jobs

Along with all of the above-mentioned bridesmaid assignments, here's what you'll be up to (give yourself some extra Bridesmaid Do-Gooder Points for each).

✦ **RINGLEADER:** It's your job to direct the other maids through their duties. You'll be making sure all the bridesmaids get their dresses, go to their dress fittings, and even find the right accessories. Sounds like a babysitter or just a total nag? Well, yeah, that's pretty much it. But it's better for you to take on that role than count on the bride to do it. You'll also give the other bridesmaids the 411 on all prewedding parties. On the wedding day, you'll see to it that they get to the wedding on time, coordinate transportation and lodging with them, if necessary, and make sure that they all get their hair and makeup done and have the correct bouquets.

SCORE: ⚐ ⚐ ⚐ ⚐ ⚐

the bride's mom is pushing her into a wedding dress she doesn't want

During a gown shopping trip, it becomes pretty clear that the mother and the bride don't share the same taste or style. If the bride falls for a silk, body-hugging sheath, but her mother is set on a gigantic princess gown, anticipate a heated discussion. If your friend is getting nowhere or she looks to you with that "sinking ship" face, by all means step in and help a bride out.

Ask her mother, "What specifically don't you like about this dress?" If she says it's "too revealing—everywhere," remember that you can negotiate just about anything, including cleavage and coverage. Perhaps the bride will wear a different bra or a corset. Maybe the dress can be let out an inch. Say, "With the veil and flowers, and with all the hugs she'll be getting, she'll be plenty covered up." Is the mother offended by the big black bow at the waist? Avoid terms like *modern* or *fashion forward*—they might scare her. Insist that it's a contemporary gown that's sure to be a classic. If she complains about the price, suggest cutting costs in other areas of the wedding, or see if the bride is willing to chip in. Finally, the bridal saleswoman should have some experience convincing mothers. Enlist her help if you need it.

✦ **GOSSIP HOUND:** Spread the news about where the bride and groom are registered.
SCORE: ⚘ ⚘ ⚘

✦ **COUNSELOR:** Lend an ear when the bride needs one. Whether it's about the planning, the marriage, or which china pattern she prefers, the MOH should assure the bride that they're in sync with each other. Even if the bride seems to dwell on the same subjects over and over and over again, the MOH keeps listening.
SCORE: ⚘ ⚘ ⚘

✦ **SECRETARY:** Not only will you host or cohost a shower for the bride, it's also customary for the MOH to be the person who keeps a record of all the gifts received at various parties and showers (or delegate the task to another maid).

SCORE: ✓ ✓

✦ **PARTY PROMOTER:** Plan the shower and the bachelorette bash with the bridesmaids.

SCORE: ✓ ✓ ✓

✦ **GUARD:** Hold the groom's ring during the ceremony if there isn't a ringbearer. (Tip: Safest place to put it? On your thumb.) You'll also hold the bride's bouquet when the couple exchanges vows.

SCORE: ✓

✦ **STYLIST:** Arrange the bride's train and veil before the ceremony begins and just after she arrives at the altar. She might also need you to help her bustle the train for easy dancing at the reception.

SCORE: ✓

✦ **OFFICIAL:** Sign the marriage license as a witness, along with the best man. You two will also dance together when the dance floor opens up to all the guests at the reception.

SCORE: ✓

ask carley

Q: Can I ask for a demotion?

A: If you think you might not be able to live up to some of the responsibilities of a maid of honor, the right thing to do is let the bride know right away. Tell her how honored you are that she picked you, but explain which part of the job you think might be tough for you (maybe it's planning the shower because you're long distance). The bride can always tweak the job description; she's the one who hired you, after all.

— HOT TOPIC —

"surprise! it's your shower!"

Okay, surprise parties are great on some occasions. We like "Surprise, happy birthday," or "Surprise, we're so happy you got that raise," or even "Surprise, we love your new place." We're not fans of the surprise wedding shower, though. There will be pictures, lots of them. The bride wants to be prepared—maybe get a blowout, buy a new top, make sure her nails are done. Give a girl some warning!

✦ **SPEECHMAKER:** Toast the couple after the best man. (This is optional but a nice touch.)

SCORE: ⚞ ⚞

✦ **BUTLER:** Make sure the top tier of the cake is saved for freezing until the bride and groom's first anniversary if they've opted to do this. And help the bride change for her honeymoon and take charge of her gown after the ceremony. You'll also be the one to arrange for it to be stored (in a safe place!) until she returns.

SCORE: ⚞ ⚞ ⚞ ⚞ ⚞ (SERIOUSLY, IF YOU ACTUALLY STORE HER DRESS, YOU'LL EARN MAJOR POINTS. THIS IS A BIG RESPONSIBILITY.)

Giving It 110%! More You Can Do

Aside from your regular maid of honor duties, you want to make this a truly special time for the bride and groom. Consider thoughtful little things you can do (water their plants while they're on their honeymoon or stock the bridal suite with their favorite snacks). They'll be so appreciative of your extra efforts. Do anything ranked five stars here, and you'll have her eternal gratitude!

✦ Take responsibility for the gift baskets or bags for out-of-town guests' hotel rooms. Include a welcome letter, maps, relevant phone numbers, snacks, postcards, city souvenirs, and suggestions for fun activities.

RATING: ★ ★ ★ ★

✦ Ask the bride when she expects the invitations to be ready and plan an informal gathering. Ask each bridesmaid to bring something to eat, crank up the tunes, and divide the duties of writing addresses, stuffing envelopes, and putting on stamps. Not only will you have fun, but you'll also be helping the bride finish a very tedious job!

RATING: ★ ★ ★ ★

✦ Offer to supply favors or place cards for the rehearsal dinner. If it's a more casual affair, offer to make simple centerpieces.

RATING: ★ ★ ★ ★ ★

✦ The perfect antidote to prewedding jitters? A great distraction. Treat the future Mr. and Mrs. to a play, concert, or great "date" movie they've been dying to see (but hadn't bought tickets for because they were too busy planning the wedding). Take the bride to get her nails done, or give her a gift certificate to her local spa for a much-needed massage.

RATING: ★ ★ ★ ★

> ── TRADITION TIDBIT ──
> *maid vs. matron*
>
> In case you were wondering what the difference is, the matron of honor is really just a maid of honor who happens to be married. Think of it as Miss versus Mrs. Some brides opt to have both a maid of honor and a matron of honor. When this happens, it's up to the bride to decide which one walks down the aisle first.

✦ A few weeks before the wedding, send guests postcards addressed to the bride, along with a letter asking them to shower her with love the week of the wedding—she'll be treated to a mailbox full of poetry, marital advice, and good wishes.

RATING: ★ ★ ★

✦ Put together a scrapbook for the bride. Begin building this book of memories when she announces her engagement. Start the book with memorabilia from where she and her sweetie met. If they're college sweethearts, frame a page in their school colors and include a photo

your job duties are growing exponentially

Figure out who's making the job overwhelming for you. If it's you pushing yourself to perfection, look for ways you can cut corners. Make a list of what you need to do, and create a realistic schedule for getting it done. Putting things down on paper helps alleviate overwhelming feelings.

If you have a long to-do list written by someone else, that's another story. Is the bride calling you every day and asking for more, more, more? Remind her what's on your plate (as far as the wedding goes and in your personal life), and say, "I honestly don't think I can do it all. What is most important to you at this very moment? I will tackle that as soon as I can." Often, she won't see how much work it is you're talking about. Be patient. Don't give her a laundry list of complaints. Simply explain that you're overwhelmed and tell her what you need (more time, more ideas, more help). And don't be a pushover if doing what she wants will cost you your health—or your friendship!

of the campus. Did he pop the question at a nearby restaurant? Pick up a matchbook and napkin to paste in. Be sure to have a camera ready to take pictures at all the prewedding parties and on the big day. Don't forget to include invitations from all the events and leave a few blank pages in the back for some of the honeymoon pictures.
RATING: ★ ★ ★ ★

✦ Give the bride a handkerchief embroidered with the happy couple's initials and their wedding date. Ask her to pass it on to the next friend who marries, embroidered with the next couple's initials and their wedding date. Eventually, your group of friends will all be married, with all your names on the hankie. So who gets it after that? The first of your children to marry.
RATING: ★ ★ ★

✦ A week or two before the wedding, help the bride get in the "wedding spirit" by decorating her home. Visit a craft store for yards of tulle, silk ivy, and lots of white faux flowers. Make swags by fastening the materials together with wire or a glue gun, and drape them along railings, around mirrors, and over doorways. Create table centerpieces by wrapping tulle around white baskets filled with some of the white flowers and use them as centerpieces. Make a white wreath or fashion a big tulle bow for the front door.
RATING: ★ ★ ★ ★

✦ The night before the wedding, give the couple a honeymoon airplane kit: towelettes, *Mad Libs*, breath mints/gum, and a stack of magazines for reading on the plane.
RATING: ★ ★ ★ ★

✦ If they're beach bound on their honeymoon, give the bride and groom matching beach totes stocked with sand-and-sun goodies: sunscreen, flip-flops, juicy beach reads, sun hats, and sunglasses—and of course, a beach blanket big enough for two.
RATING: ★ ★ ★ ★

✦ Ask what the bride's drinking at the reception and keep her glass full. Brides seldom make it through the crowd to the bar.
RATING: ★ ★ ★

The BEST Bridesmaid

✦ Offer to be the end-of-the-party/final once-over girl: Collect the cake topper and toasting flutes, make sure Grandma is escorted to her car, and so on.

RATING: ★ ★ ★ ★ ★

✦ Stock the couple's kitchen with food for their return. What could be worse than having to go to the grocery store the night you return from paradise? Help them avoid reality for just one more day.

RATING: ★ ★ ★ ★

Bridesmaids Who Went Beyond

Want to get some good ideas from bridesmaids who really took their job seriously and cranked it up a notch?

"I got the bride an MP3 player to use on her long flight to Hawaii for the honeymoon. I filled it with lots of love songs, sexy 'honeymoon' music, and fun tunes I knew she loved when we were in high school—like songs by Duran Duran and the theme to *The Breakfast Club*." —debeatle

"I was the maid of honor for my sister's wedding, and I offered to take all the wedding checks to the bank and deposit them in the couple's account. When they got back from their honeymoon, the checks had all cleared and they had a nice little nest egg." —rachelb23

"I had cute matching T-shirts made for their honeymoon that said, 'Announcing the New Mr. and Mrs. K.' They wore the shirts on their honeymoon cruise and everyone gave them special treatment."

—sapsmass781

WHERE TO CLICK: Did we mention you *also* need to be up on what's hot in weddings? Subscribe to The Knot wedding style blog at TheKnot.com/weddingstyle.

CHAPTER TWO

play nice

chances are you've met at least one other person in the bridal party before the nuptial festivities begin, but you'll have to talk with everyone in the group at some point. One of your duties as an attendant is to help ensure harmony within the wedding party. It's important not to let little splinter groups form—the fam, the high school friends, the college friends . . . you get the picture. These mini cliques can equal big problems if people feel left out, or if all of a sudden shower planning, bachelorette parties, or fittings turn into a big "us" against "them" situation. Besides, you'll have more fun participating in all the prewedding activities if you're comfortable with the rest of the group and if you make an effort to be friendly. And you'll be taking the pressure off the bride. She's in the position of having to introduce friends from all areas of her life and hoping they get along, which, in this case, is like setting up a blind date and then actually going along on the date to make sure they really like each other! Talk about awkward.

you first meet the other bridesmaids

To start things off on the right foot, keep it simple, light, and upbeat. Introduce yourself with your name, where you live, and how you know the bride. Avoid saying, "I'm her best friend in the whole world," in case there's a childhood friend who also thinks she has the same title. Just say, "I was good friends with [insert bride's name here] in graduate school. How do you know the bride?"

And then say, "It's so neat to meet someone from her past. So you grew up in Cincinnati as well! Did you really let her sleep over during thunderstorms, like she said?" You can tell her, "I've heard such wonderful things about you," if it's at least somewhat true and you sound genuine saying it! Practicing these niceties will help for the wedding day in case you need to take the bride's great-aunt to the bathroom or mix it up with strangers at the cocktail hour.

Bonding with Your Fellow Bridesmaids

If a bunch of you live near one another, organize a little meet-and-greet, with or without the bride. Get together for brunch or cocktails and exchange phone numbers, addresses, emails, even measurements (you'll need them if just one of you is ordering everyone's gowns). Use the form on page 33. Now's a good time to discuss how you'll communicate, how often, and who will be in charge of getting the word out. You can also ask if anyone has any special talents: Maybe someone is a whiz at calligraphy and can address envelopes, while another is an amateur chef and wants to cater the shower. Be honest about how much time and money you have to contribute to the wedding.

If there are long-distance bridesmaids, make sure you get their info as well, and take note of any special needs they might have (finding a hotel for the wedding, getting dresses shipped and fitted, arranging transportation or carpooling for prewedding events). Mostly, you don't

want anyone to feel out of the loop just because she lives in another town. So email, connect on Facebook, Twitter your updates, or create your own bridesmaid blog.

10 Things Never to Say to the Other Bridesmaids

1. "Oh, I didn't realize you'd be one of the bridesmaids. I know [insert bride's name] was having such a difficult time choosing whom to include."

2. "[Insert bride's name] told me she'd help me pay for my dress if I keep it on the DL. But you should ask her, too—what have you got to lose?"

3. "I hate weddings."

4. "Wow, I didn't know you knew how to do that ceremonial dance. Would you mind performing it at my wedding, too?"

5. "What kind of dress silhouette do you usually wear? We have such different figures—it will be hard to find one style that works on everyone."

6. "It's nice that even though you guys have grown apart, you're still willing to be a bridesmaid."

7. "If you lose like five or ten pounds, this dress will look amazing on you."

8. "[Insert bride's name]'s fiancé is hot—we dated for a brief period of time before they met."

9. "Since I'm flying to the wedding from out of state, I have to pay for long-distance travel on top of everything else. Do you think you could pitch in extra for some of our shared bridesmaid costs?"

10. "Why is she getting married before me?"

Now, Let's Behave

Usually, most of the attendants are eager to pitch in and work together. But occasionally, you'll find some "problems" in the bunch—a bridesmaid who simply prefers to march to her own beat, loves to be argumentative, or doesn't play well with others. Or maybe it's not even your fellow bridesmaids who are rocking the boat. Perhaps it's the mother of the bride who's making trouble, or even someone who wasn't picked to be in the wedding party. Tread lightly with these types. They thrive on creating confusion and chaos—which is exactly what you want to avoid. Rather than ignore the person and let those bad vibes envelop everyone and everything, nip the problem in the bud. Try these constructive responses.

Invitation Drama

✦ **IF A BRIDESMAID SAYS . . .** "Since I live far away and won't be attending the bridal shower, I don't want to be listed on the invitation as cohostess. I also don't want to pay for my share of hosting it."

✦ **YOU SAY . . .** "Please reconsider. We all want to support her as one solid group. Besides, the bride will think of you as in attendance since you'll be there in spirit!"

Bridesmaid Cheat Sheet

At some point—sooner rather than later—you'll need to have all this info on hand. Have each bridesmaid fill out the following form. Each of you can keep the info in a computer file (one person can type it up and email it out), in a three-ring binder, even on index cards in a recipe box, whatever is easiest, just as long as everyone has a master list to refer to.

Bridesmaid's name: . . . .

Home phone number: . . . .

Mobile phone: . . . .

Email address: . . . .

Address: . . . .

Fax/other numbers: . . . .

Measurements:

      Chest: . . . .

      Waist: . . . .

      Hips: . . . .

Usual dress size:. . . . .

Shoe size:. . . . .

Additional notes (spouse's/children's names; special talents; conditions/allergies to flowers, food, etc., that might impact the wedding):

. . . .
. . . .
. . . .
. . . .
. . . .

one of your fellow bridesmaids gets dumped right before the wedding

Ask her about her feelings. Is she resentful? Despondent? Shocked? Immobile? Sad? Now's the time for understanding but also tough love. Tell her she'll have to put her feelings aside and look at the bride's day as an isolated event, which is outside of her feelings about romance, men, marriage, diamond rings, and so forth. Ask her to put herself in the bride's shoes. It's not her fault that she just happens to be marrying *now*, so it's best to keep a stiff upper lip and be happy for her. Reassure the bridesmaid that the bride *does* have every sympathy for her friend, but she also wants to stay away from sad feelings on her wedding day—and it's nothing personal. The bride is probably so stressed out that it may not seem like she can give this situation all of her attention. She will probably shut it out—which might look insensitive. Tell your friend that this is another time to suck it up: "Try not to envy the bride and just know that the minute she returns from her honeymoon, she'll be happy to be the shoulder you cry on."

Shower Power Struggle

✦ **IF THE MOTHER OF THE BRIDE SAYS . . .** "Don't bother planning the bridal shower—I'll do it because I just remodeled my home and it's great for parties. Besides, all my friends want to come."

✦ **YOU SAY . . .** "Oh, that's very generous of you! Have you discussed this with your daughter? I want to make sure she's in the loop about everything—like the size and location of the shower. Surprises at a time like this might be a little unnerving for her."

Dress Stress

✦ **IF THE BRIDE SAYS . . .** "I really want champagne-colored dresses, but so-and-so says champagne won't look good with her skin tone. I know it's my day, but I want all my bridesmaids to be happy, especially since they're paying for their own dresses and shoes."

✦ **YOU SAY . . .** "That's very nice of you to consider her feelings about the dress color, but you're right—it's your day. She can pick the color you'll wear at *her* wedding. For now, you just can't please everyone. Remind her that we'll be a cohesive and beautiful group when we stand together beside you on your wedding day. If you feel uncomfortable, would you like me to speak to her for you? I won't mention we had this specific conversation."

Meet the Bridesmaids!

Here's the cast of characters you might encounter as a bridesmaid, plus some smart strategies for dealing with them. Watch out—and pull it together if any of these sounds like you!

The Bossy Bridesmaid

✦ **HOW TO SPOT HER:** Her motto is "It's my way or the highway." She knows everything and does everything better than you (just ask her!), and she isn't interested in hearing anyone else's opinion. Maybe the bride put her in charge and all that power has gone to her head.

Why don't I go first!

✦ **HOW TO HANDLE HER:** You want to deal with this maidzilla tactfully. A little ego stroking can't hurt ("Your idea is brilliant! But how about if we try it this way . . ."). Or you can gently remind her that this isn't a dictatorship.

✦ **IF YOU ARE HER:** Of course, you're just being organized, on top if it, and responsible. We know. But it's okay to let go a little bit; in fact, it would be welcome. This wedding is supposed to be fun, and you shouldn't treat it like it's a project for work. No one will give you a promotion for coming up with a brilliant shower invite, but the other girls might alienate you if they think you're ignoring all of their ideas.

The Reluctant Bridesmaid

✦ **HOW TO SPOT HER:** She makes it pretty clear that she's none too thrilled to be here.

✦ **HOW TO HANDLE HER:** It's never a good solution to ignore and exclude her (although it's tempting). Instead, assure her that she's both wanted and needed. If she still protests, then assign her some tasks that don't require people skills. Maybe she can stuff envelopes or tally up response cards.

✦ **IF YOU ARE HER:** What's the deal? Are you really unenthused about being in the bridal party? If you are, then you've got to suck it up. You'd want someone else to do the same for you.

The Wannabe Bridesmaid

✦ **HOW TO SPOT HER:** This is the girl who wasn't picked but clearly thinks it must have been an oversight. She's even asked you what the bridesmaids will be wearing so she can buy the same dress.

✦ **HOW TO HANDLE HER:** If she looks like a bridesmaid, she might be treated like one, and it's very expensive to have the photographer edit someone out of a group shot. So get this girl in line well before the wedding. Yes, it will be uncomfortable to say, "Um, you know, those dresses are for the girls in the bridal party, and since you're actually not, it would be a little weird for you to wear the same thing." But you've just got to do it. The longer you wait, the more awkward the conversation will be.

✦ **IF YOU ARE HER:** Remind yourself how difficult it is for a bride to decide on her bridal party and don't take it so personally. We understand it feels personal, but you have no idea what's going through her mind. Maybe she thinks if she includes you that means she'll have to include her three other high school friends, or maybe she's set on having an even number on both sides, and the groom doesn't have anyone else he wants to add. If you're truly a friend, you'll respect the decision she made. Case closed.

The Pregnant Bridesmaid

✦ **HOW TO SPOT HER:** She's worried about spilling out of a strapless gown and is very leery about wearing heels.

✦ **HOW TO HANDLE HER:** Even if you suspect she's pregnant, you have to wait until she announces it before you say anything. But it's not a bad idea to suggest a dress with an Empire waist if the bride is open to ideas.

✦ **IF YOU ARE HER:** Don't just mysteriously bow out; tell the bride as soon as possible and let her decide how she wants to deal. Chances are she won't mind. But it might affect the dress style. If you've tried on the dress and there's just no way you'll be able to wear it (if it has a band around the waist, for example), tell the bride you'll find another style in the same color and fabric that will work.

The Broke Bridesmaid

✦ **HOW TO SPOT HER:** She's out of work, has college loans to repay, and doesn't have any idea how she'll cover next month's rent—much less the cost of a bridesmaid dress and all the extras. You ask her for $20 toward a shower gift and she replies, "Would you take an IOU?"

✦ **HOW TO HANDLE HER:** Don't make her feel worse about her financial situation by asking her to go in with you on gifts. She might not want to spend as much, and you don't want to be in a position of subsidizing for her. If she can't afford the dress, it's up to her, not you, to take it up with the bride.

✦ **IF YOU ARE HER:** Help out in ways that don't cost money. Offer to be the organizer for the group; volunteer your time and talents. Don't turn it into a big issue because it really isn't, and you'll just make everyone feel uncomfortable.

The Jealous Bridesmaid

✦ **HOW TO SPOT HER:** She's irritating everyone with her pettiness. Why isn't *she* the one walking down the aisle? Why isn't this *her* wedding you're planning? She's bitter, even a bit vindictive (she thought it would be fun to put the bride's naked baby picture on the shower invite).

✦ **HOW TO HANDLE HER:** Reassure her that her day will come. Commiserate. Promise to introduce her to all the cute single men at the wedding. Do whatever it takes to keep this nastiness from surfacing.

✦ **IF YOU ARE HER:** Repeat after us, "This is not my wedding. This is not about me. It will be my turn one day [or it has already been my turn]."

Now, refocus that energy on doing a great job for the bride. She'll owe you one later.

The Out-of-Town Bridesmaid

✦ **HOW TO SPOT HER:** It's easy! She lives across the country or on another continent. Although she wants to be helpful, she's not able to attend a lot of the prewedding festivities or physically pitch in with any errands or tasks.

✦ **HOW TO HANDLE HER:** Keep her in the loop and give her some suggestions on how she can contribute. Maybe she can send flowers to the shower or engagement party or chip in on the group gift. Maybe she has some old photos of the bride you can use for a slide show or scrapbook. Out of sight shouldn't mean out of mind—especially if she's ready and willing to do her part.

✦ **IF YOU ARE HER:** Acknowledge all the work the other bridesmaids are doing and make an effort to contribute long-distance.

The Break-the-Rules Bridesmaid

✦ **HOW TO SPOT HER:** She's got fuchsia hair, a nose ring, and head-to-toe tattoos—and she insists this is how she'll walk down the aisle. When you show her the powder-pink taffeta bridesmaid dress everyone is going to wear, she asks if she can dye it black.

✦ **HOW TO HANDLE HER:** As long as the bride doesn't mind her maid's "different" style (she knew what she was getting into when she asked her), you shouldn't either. If the bride does have an issue, but doesn't want to be the bad guy, you need to say something. Tell the renegade maid that the bride wants you all to stick to the style she's picked. It might even make her feel better if you let her know it's not your preference either, but as bridesmaids you all need to suck it up for your friend.

✦ **IF YOU ARE HER:** Don't freak out the other bridesmaids with off-the-wall requests. If there's something you feel strongly about, like wearing pants instead of a dress, go straight to the bride and then tell the other girls what you and she decided. They don't need to cast their vote on these issues; it's between you and the woman of the hour.

The Male Maid

✦ **HOW TO SPOT HIM:** He's the guy. While he's being a sport, all the girls are grumbling about having a guy in their circle and making him feel unwelcome.

✦ **HOW TO HANDLE HIM:** Come on, the tension isn't his fault. He didn't ask to be an "intruder" in your midst. Maybe he's not going to get giddy over gowns or dwell on the steamy details of the bachelorette bash, but maybe he is, so make sure you invite him to your activities and let him decide if he wants to participate. You might be surprised by how nice it is to have a guy's perspective now and then.

✦ **IF YOU ARE HIM:** We're *so* impressed you're reading this book.

The Bossy Bridesman

✦ **HOW TO SPOT HIM:** You hear him before you see him because his opinionated voice is even louder than his flashy clothes. (Okay, we're being a bit stereotypical here, but we speak from experience.) He tells the bride what colors are most flattering and what shoes the girls should wear, and he's the only one of you who knew exactly what cymbidium orchids looked like. The bride trusts his opinion and has no time for yours.

✦ **HOW TO HANDLE HIM:** You'll have to be firm. A bossy bridesman will not want to be told what to do. Your best defense is calling for group consensus when he throws out his ideas (and he will). Make it clear that you're interested in everyone's opinion, not just his. If he rolls his eyes, tell him you don't appreciate the attitude. (Yes, channel your mother.)

✦ **IF YOU ARE HIM:** Remember that you are not the only person in the bridal party (even if you happen to be the one with the best taste).

The Other Troublemakers

Every wedding—and every family—has 'em: people whose personalities make your life difficult. As time draws nearer to the wedding day, more and more of these characters will pop up. So prepare yourself now for any scenario, especially because a few tenacious busybodies may actually create problems as early as the engagement party. Here's how to deal.

The Meddlesome Mother of the Bride (or the Overbearing Mom-in-Law)

✦ **HOW TO SPOT HER:** She's got her nose in every detail of her daughter's day. Any plans require her sign-off and approval. She's vetoed your gowns (twice!), nixed umbrella centerpieces at the shower ("Tacky!"), and insists on "editing" the bride and groom's registry.

✦ **HOW TO HANDLE HER:** Well, if the bride's (or groom's) parents are paying for the whole wedding, this woman is technically the hostess of the party, so you've got to cut her some slack. But being the official hostess and driving the bride crazy are two different things. The trick is to set some ground rules without causing World War III Practice the art of compromise (maybe you'll agree to a chocolate fountain at the bachelorette party if she'll ease up on the bridesmaid dress style). Be polite and respectful, even if it means biting your tongue. Thank the mother of the bride for her input, her wisdom, and her attention to detail (*every* detail!). Come up with a plan: Maybe there are some tasks she'd be happy to delegate. Maybe all she's really asking for is to be kept in the loop. And just remember: This dictatorship is only temporary. Luckily, she's not your mom.

The Annoying Invitee

✦ **HOW TO SPOT HER:** Thanks to the phone number you provided with the RSVP for the shower invite, she has you on speed dial. She has a million questions and is delighted to find someone in the "inner circle" who can fill her in. She wants to know what to buy the bride ("Towels? China? A cappuccino maker? I just can't decide!"), what's on the menu (she's allergic to shellfish), and if the hotel she'll be staying at allows pets (she can't bear to leave her precious pup at home).

✦ **HOW TO HANDLE HER:** Take a deep breath and don't lose your temper. She clearly cares about the wedding (this is a good thing), even if she's irritatingly inquisitive. Explain that you're very busy with planning and helping the bride, and although you'd love to, you're not always available to chat. Give her the address for the couple's wedding web page so she can find some of the answers there, or suggest that she email you a list of her questions and you'll respond ASAP. If all else fails, screen your calls.

The Guest "Plus One"

✦ **HOW TO SPOT HER:** This person insists on bringing extra baggage (and we don't mean luggage) to every event. She asks if she can take her toddler to the bachelorette party ("I can't get a sitter that night"), and if it's not too much of a bother, she'll be bringing her boyfriend of two weeks to the all-girl shower ("I really need a ride and I'm dying for him to meet everyone!").

✦ **HOW TO HANDLE HER:** Call her and explain that the guest list for the get-together is already at the max. Don't feel guilty. Let her decide if it means she'll have to decline the invite or make other arrangements. Besides, if you allow her to bring someone, you'll have to bend the rules for others as well. Stand your ground—just do so politely.

Rumor Patrol

You know that old game of Telephone where one person tells the next person something, then she passes it on to a third person, and so on? Well, as a bridesmaid, you want to avoid this game. Yes, everyone needs to be in the loop, but there are right and wrong ways to chitchat with the rest of the bridal party. The fastest way to spread misinformation is to rely on a phone tree, where individuals either leave out details or pass on the wrong facts. It's best to have just one person in charge of correspondence; she can send information up or down a chain or write one mass email.

SHE DID WHAT?

bridesmaids behaving badly

When I found a bridesmaid dress online that I loved, I emailed the link to the group. I wasn't pushy at all, I just asked them to check it out and also take a look at the model's hair—I liked that, too. But one of my bridesmaids wrote a long diatribe intended for the other girls about how ugly the dress was and basically what a bridezilla I was. I got the email, too. She accidentally hit "reply all." Needless to say, I relieved her of her services. —kit10023

10 Basic Rules of Communication

Not sure what's appropriate and don't want to come across as too pushy or too lazy? Follow these tips.

✦ **DON'T LEAVE ANYONE OUT:** Set up a group with all the bridesmaids' addresses, or friend each other on Facebook so you can communicate together.

✦ **GET TO THE POINT:** Don't send a long-winded email that goes off on several tangents. Organize it into concise, specific points so the message is clear.

✦ **EDIT YOURSELF:** Sending a few photos of possible dresses is okay; an entire catalog's worth isn't. You can always forward a link to the designer you love.

✦ **ACT NORMAL:** ALL CAPS, tons of smileys, exclamation points, and boldface type can be annoying. Keep your emails simple.

✦ **BE SMART:** Don't spill private info. If one bridesmaid has confided something, don't send it around to the entire group. Be respectful of people's privacy and mindful of your own. If one of the bridesmaids needs your credit card, call her with the number.

✦ **STICK TO BUSINESS:** No sending around chain letters, ads, jokes, or other unsolicited info (unless your pals tell you it's okay).

✦ **RATION "REPLY ALL":** If one bridesmaid asks you a specific question, you don't need to answer it for all to see.

✦ **CHANNEL YOUR ENGLISH TEACHER:** Use proper spelling, grammar, and punctuation. Sure, mistakes happen in haste, but you want to communicate clearly as well as respect every bridesmaid by getting the spelling of her name correctly. Also, some of the girls may have given you their work email addresses, so be careful with the language you use—some corporations heavily monitor or filter email correspondence, and your oh-so-important message could be lost to an individual's trash or spam folder.

✦ **DON'T BE AN ALARMIST:** Avoid using URGENT and IMPORTANT in the subject, unless the message truly is. Remember the boy who cried wolf: If you keep labeling everything with exclamation points, then no one will pay attention when a real urgent issue arises.

✦ **CENSOR YOURSELF:** If you have anything on your Facebook or MySpace pages or in your blog that you don't want the others to see—like a complaint about any one of them or the bride—remove it. You probably shouldn't have posted it in the first place.

 WHERE TO CLICK: You likely have it better than most! Console other bridesmaids or be consoled on The Knot message boards: TheKnot.com/boards.

CHAPTER THREE
get your wallet ready

being a bridesmaid is a big honor, and it usually comes with a pretty big price tag, too. You will wind up spending several hundred—if not a few thousand—dollars by the time everything is said and done. We're going to be really blunt here: Don't bitch about it. There is no need to rant about how much you're spending to the other bridesmaids, and especially not to the bride. It's just rude. The good news is that once you know what to expect, you can budget early and keep an eye on your wallet. And remember, this isn't money you're going to be spending all at once. From the time you buy that first engagement gift to the moment you send off your credit-card payment with the flight, hotel, and wedding-gift charges, we're probably talking six to eight months. But it's smart to know what to expect right from the get-go. And, there are some areas you might not be so sure about, like transportation to the wedding (yep, that's you) or the bridesmaids' luncheon (you're off the hook here).

The Bridesmaid Bill

Here's a rundown of the things you'll probably be expected to pay for.

✦ Accommodation for and transportation to the wedding (if applicable) $$$$

✦ Your dress, shoes, accessories, hair, and makeup $$$

✦ The bridal shower and bachelorette party $$

✦ Wedding and bridal shower gifts $$

Not on My Tab

Now that you know what you'll have to shell out for, here are a few of the biggies you don't have to worry about financing.

✦ The bridesmaid bouquets

✦ The rehearsal dinner

✦ The bridesmaids' luncheon (Note: This is different from the shower and is hosted by the bride.)

SHE DID WHAT?

brides behaving badly

"She wanted all of the bridesmaids to buy matching clutches. Cute, but they never carried them down the aisle because they had bouquets. They were just for show at the reception!" —banana468

Tallying Up Your Tab

Use these figures as a guesstimate for what the wedding will cost you and as a guide for how to allocate your funds. Keep receipts and careful records of how much you're spending. Sometimes, over several months, it's easy to lose perspective, forget what you've already paid for, and blow your budget without even realizing it. You're excited, swept up in the moment, and thinking, *Oh my gosh! Those shoes are to die for!* But so were those earrings three months ago, and the beaded handbag two months before that. The goal is to avoid shopping amnesia. In a small notebook, write down how much you can afford to spend, and deduct the cost of each item you buy. Then you'll know what you have left and when it's okay to give in to that impulse purchase. Here's what you can expect to spend on each must-have bridesmaid item.

i saved!

"My roommate was in a wedding a few weeks after me, and we both needed something simple and black, so we found this great dress, and fortunately, it fit both of us. Each of us paid half for it, plus the cost of dry cleaning after I wore it to the wedding. It's pretty funny. We now say we have 'joint custody' of it." —teacherreb79

✦ **BRIDESMAID DRESS:** $100–$700. This is a biggie, and usually you'll be expected to pay for it on your own. Hopefully, the bride will choose something reasonable that you can wear again or she'll consider letting you pick your own dress. She may give you color and/or style requirements (for example, black and ankle length) and then ask each bridesmaid to select something that suits her own style, body, and budget. We'll get into more detail on this in chapter 4.

✦ **EVERYTHING THAT GOES WITH THE DRESS (SHOES, LINGERIE, JEWELRY, HAIR, AND MAKEUP):** $325–$1,050. We'll break these down more in chapter 4. But for now, just remember that these MVEs (most valuable extras) really do add up, maybe costing you more than the dress itself. Sometimes, the bride will ask you to buy very specific items—see She Did What? on page 52.

the bride decides on designer bridesmaid dresses that cost $1,000 each

Even if all the other bridesmaids appear to be able to afford an insane price, don't give in! You must speak up. We give you permission. Don't go to the other bridesmaids and gossip—go straight to the bride. (And don't fire off a long, angry text.) Call her and say, "I understand why you love this dress! But I have to be honest—it's way beyond my price range. I haven't talked to the other girls, but I'm sure they feel the same way, especially those who also have to travel a long distance for your wedding. I looked online and emailed you a few links to dresses that look similar but cost less. Or perhaps we could ask a dressmaker to create the same design but in a more economical fabric? I'm sorry—I won't be drawing any other boundaries on your special day, but I have budgeted for no more than [insert price] for the dress."

You don't have to say *all* of that, but use this quote as your guideline. Acknowledge her choice, and don't tell her you're shocked by the price or her audacious request that you pay for it. Don't say she's crazy or selfish. But do be sure to give her a maximum number you are willing to spend; otherwise, she might "back off" and choose a dress that's $899. Then present her with alternatives and options. Remember: "Diplomacy" is your middle name!

✦ **TRAVEL AND ACCOMMODATION:** $200–$1,000+. Depending on how far you have to go and your method of transport (plane, train, or automobile), this could end up being your biggest expense. Besides the transportation, consider what other costs you'll have to incur: hotel, car rental, getting to and from the airport, and so on. Usually, the bride and groom reserve a block of rooms at a group price in a reasonable hotel close to the reception site.

✦ **THE SHOWER:** $50–$200. Whoever is hosting the shower (usually the maid of honor with help from the bridesmaids) should foot the bill. See more details in chapter 5.

✦ **GIFT FOR THE SHOWER:** $30–$60. Yep, even if you're the one hosting the shower, you still have to buy the bride a present. Stick to the 20-20-60 rule: Spend 20 percent of your gift budget on the shower, 20 percent on the engagement gift, and 60 percent on the wedding gift. It's a good idea to buy off her registry, too, so you know it's exactly what she wants. We'll get more into great gift ideas in chapter 5.

✦ **GIFT FOR THE WEDDING:** $90–$180+. Sure, it's the thought that counts, but since you're a member of the wedding party, you'll probably want to buy the bride and groom something special. If you are trying to keep costs down, buy off the registry early when the good high-value, lower-priced items are still there. And yes, giving money is totally acceptable. In fact, some couples even prefer it. If you gift them a check, just be sure you make it out to the right name if the bride is changing hers, or keep it simple and make it out to "Cash."

✦ **BACHELORETTE PARTY:** $50–$200. The cost of the bachelorette party is traditionally split among the bridesmaids, including the maid of honor and often the other attendees, which should keep your contribution reasonable.

i got creative

"I knew the bride collected Barbie dolls when she was little, so we went on eBay, got a bunch of inexpensive Barbies, and sewed little white bridal gowns and veils from some inexpensive cotton fabric and tulle. We used them as centerpieces all over the room. Her face when she walked in was priceless." —rdol

brides behaving badly

"She made the entire bridal party buy $300 sundresses for the rehearsal dinner—in addition to the $400 bridesmaid dresses they'd already purchased. Outrageous!" —kello16

Top 10 Ways to Save

So now that you've got the gist of what this is going to cost you, we bet you'd love some savings tricks, wouldn't you?

✦ **SAVE ON SHIPPING.** If possible, have all smaller items (shoes and accessories) mailed to one address (maybe the maid of honor's) to save on shipping costs. Sometimes with a big order, shipping is free!

✦ **SAVE ON HAIRSTYLING.** When girls get together, great hairstyles can happen. Throw a "Do My Do" party! Try out different styles—you'll have fun and save a bundle at the salon. Even if you end up going to a pro, you won't have to waste money on a trial run.

✦ **SAVE ON YOUR FLIGHT.** Make your plane reservation as early as possible to get the best rates.

i saved!

"I found the gravy boat my friend registered for on a discount website for 40 percent less, plus free shipping. Then I just called the registry and had the item removed ('purchased elsewhere') so they didn't receive a double." —mcsher2

✦ **SAVE ON TRAVEL AND LODGING.** Split costs wherever you can: Carpool, share a taxi, ask if you can go halvsies on a hotel room with one of the bridesmaids or another single guest.

✦ **SAVE ON SHOWER DECORATIONS.** Instead of buying or renting shower

Q: Is it okay to charge per head at a bachelorette party, or do the maid of honor and bridesmaids foot the bill for everything?

A: Unlike the shower, where the party is hosted and paid for by only the maid of honor or by all the bridesmaids, it's fine to ask everyone who comes to chip in for the bachelorette bash. And everyone chips in the same amount—whether they're part of the wedding party or not. But make this clear before the festivities begin. Inform all invitees what the plan is and how much the suggested contribution will be. No one should have a problem with it—everyone wants to feel like she's showing the bride a good time.

decorations and favors, do them yourself. Make it a fun get-together project, putting everyone's talents to work. Balloons and streamers are festive yet inexpensive, and you can make your own "wishing well" out of cardboard. Chapter 5 provides lots of creative ideas.

✦ **SAVE ON THE WEDDING GIFT.** Watch for discounts at stores where the bride and groom are registered. It's not uncommon for whole china collections to go on sale a few times throughout the year.

✦ **SAVE ON SHOWER INVITES.** Make these a DIY project or shop online for printers that will customize an invitation for a lot less than it would cost if you went to a traditional stationery company.

✦ **SAVE ON THE BACHELORETTE PARTY.** Kick off the bash at someone's place—or even have the whole event there. Bring entertainment, but buy your own booze. See chapter 6 for ideas.

✦ **SAVE ON ALTERATIONS.** Buy your undergarments before you go for the fitting. It can really affect the tailoring, and this will save you from having to do it twice.

Look on the bright side. Even though you may have to shell out a few hundred dollars for your dress, it could be worse. Centuries ago, all the bridesmaids had to wear the exact same thing as the bride. Yes, that's right, if there had been a Vera Wang–type wedding gown designer back then, and that's what the bride chose, the bridesmaids would have had to buy the same dress. Sound strange? The reason is that people believed the bride and groom would be protected from being cursed if the evil spirits couldn't figure out exactly who was getting married.

✦ **NEGOTIATE** a good makeup price by getting all of the bridesmaids together.

The Tough Talk

If you're in a situation where you know you can't afford to be a bridesmaid, it's better to tell the bride right off the bat. Don't be embarrassed; not everyone has an unlimited bank account (although some of the other girls in the bridal party may seem to). Be honest about what you can and can't afford.

Chances are you're not the only one among the attendants concerned about money. Together you can come up with some solutions.

WHERE TO CLICK: New saving tricks are being dreamed up daily! For more bridesmaid budget advice see our money channel, TheKnot.com/budgeting.

My Bridesmaid Budget

ITEM/ACTIVITY	ESTIMATED COST	ACTUAL COST
Bridesmaid dress	$100–$700	
Lingerie	$80–$150	
Shoes	$50–$400+	
Jewelry	$50–$200+	
Hair	$50–$200	
Makeup	$70–$150	
Travel/accommodations	$200–$1,000+	
Shower	$50–$200	
Shower gift	$30–$60	
Engagement gift	$30–$60	
Wedding gift	$90–$180+	
Bachelorette party	$50–$200	
TOTAL	**$875–$3,750**	

NOTES:

CHAPTER FOUR
you'll love the dress

yes, we've all heard those dress horror stories. You think she's your best friend—that's why she asked you to be in her bridal party, right? But then she sends you the link to a bubble-gum-pink, floor-length satin dress that shows every little bulge, not to mention bra and underwear lines. For a second, you figure she's joking. "Ha-ha . . . very funny. Now where's the real dress?" you say to yourself. You read the subject line of the email: "I love this. What do you think?" Uh-oh. Now you're convinced she has been holding a secret grudge against you since seventh grade when you kissed her boyfriend and has been waiting for the perfect revenge. Well, here's a news flash: Even though you're the one who has to wear the bridesmaid dress, it's actually not about you. We know . . . shocker! For her, the dress is an extension of the rest of the wedding details. This isn't to say she doesn't care if you don't like it; but the real reason it has a scoop neckline is probably because she thinks it's highlighting the shape of the calla lilies you'll be holding, not because you and her sister both have great cleavage.

Don't let this news make you panic. Trust us—it's really unlikely you'll be forced to wear pink and purple argyle if the invitations are trimmed with that pattern. We just wanted to give you some perspective on where she's coming from. The good news is designers have gotten the message about ugly bridesmaid dresses, and more pretty, flattering, wearable styles are available than ever before. This means that the chances of your getting stuck with a doozy are actually pretty low. As far as being able to wear it again, well . . . that's a different story.

How to Get What You Want (Nicely)

To make sure it's a win-win situation, practice some smart tactics. Start looking at dresses *before* the bride does. It's much easier to point her in the direction of something you like than to dissuade her from something she's already picked out. As soon as she asks you to be in her bridal party, begin browsing. Here's how to sneak in your opinion without making it seem like you're being a maidzilla.

Top 5 Things to Say to Get Her to Like the Same Dress You Do

1. "Too bad you can't pick this! Your future mother-in-law [or mother or whoever is giving her a harder time with the details] would hate it."

WHY IT WORKS: Can you say, Score one for the bride? This is a battle she knows she can win.

2. "This dress is nice because it will blend in with everything else; we won't stand out too much."

WHY IT WORKS: This one's easy; she wants the attention on her. It's *her* wedding, after all.

3. "Everyone looks good in [insert color]."

WHY IT WORKS: Basically, you're assuring her that no one in the bridal party will be able to complain about the hue.

4. "This style is really [insert whatever adjectives she's been using to describe the wedding—modern, autumnal, chic, etc.]!"

WHY IT WORKS: Even if it's a stretch, she wants to believe all the elements of the wedding are working together. Grecian gown = preppy? Well, maybe not, but if you really, really like the dress, you might be able to make her think it does.

5. "You won't even be able to tell [fill in the person's name] is pregnant in this."

WHY IT WORKS: If the dress can hide a *baby*, no one else can complain that it makes her look fat. Also, it goes back to that idea of the bride wanting the attention on her, not on her pregnant friend.

Now, how about when she sends you the pictures of what she's thinking about? Remember the bright-pink, floor-length number? Hopefully, you know you can't just say, "It's hideous and I'm not wearing that." So what *can* you say? Anything? Yes, but this definitely requires some finessing.

10 Ways to Say "I Hate It"—Without Saying "I Hate It"

1. "Oh, wait, I think I'm looking at the wrong one. I only see the long, satin, hot-pink dress here. [Pause.] Is that the one?"

THE SCIENCE BEHIND IT: The trick here is not to put emphasis on any word in that last sentence. "*Is* that the one?" says: "I'm trying not to be judgmental, but seriously, *that's* it?" Change the emphasis to "Is *that* the one?" and you're saying: "I'm not even going to pretend I think that's cute. Have you lost your mind?"

2. "Hot pink? That's a strong color."

THE SCIENCE BEHIND IT: Notice the use of the word *strong;* it's not quite as harsh as *hideous.*

3. "It's so pretty, but it might be a little too [insert adjective] for [insert another girl from the bridal party] to pull off."

THE SCIENCE BEHIND IT: You're just looking out for the other girls. Wink, wink.

4. "Oh yeah, I've seen that style everywhere. I know exactly what you're talking about."

THE SCIENCE BEHIND IT: Reverse psychology: The bride *wants* her wedding to be like everyone else's, right?

5. "I love it, but do you think it will match [fill in anything: the flowers, the groomsmen's looks, the cake]?"

THE SCIENCE BEHIND IT: It really doesn't have to make sense; the goal is to make the bride feel less confident in her decision.

6. "Is that supposed to be tea length, or does it just look like it on that model?"

THE SCIENCE BEHIND IT: The bride is already questioning everything and wondering if she's making the right choices. If you make her think there's something strange about the hemline, she'll want to keep looking for a dress that's perfect.

7. "It reminds me so much of the dress we wore for [insert name]'s wedding."

THE SCIENCE BEHIND IT: Again, the bride *wants* her wedding to be like everyone else's, right?

8. "Nice. I wonder if you can get it without the crinoline, too?"

THE SCIENCE BEHIND IT: This is just a polite way of saying, "That crinoline looks really bad." And it gives the bride a way to easily save face. If the dress is available without the crinoline, she knows that's what her bridesmaids prefer and might be willing to concede.

9. "Wow, it's beautiful, but I thought your wedding was going to be more casual."

THE SCIENCE BEHIND IT: This seemingly innocuous comment will give her an instant reality check: Maybe this dress really doesn't work with the rest of her wedding style?

10. "Look at that; it even comes with dyed-to-match shoes. That's good because I wouldn't have any idea what shoes to wear with that shade of . . . fuchsia, is it?" Tip: Try to say this with genuine enthusiasm. She'll get the point and it won't sound so mean.

THE SCIENCE BEHIND IT: Most brides want the bridesmaid dresses to reflect the wedding's color scheme. If she's afraid you can't figure out the color of your dress, she'll worry that the other guests won't be able to either.

The ultimate decision is the bride's (you did know that, right?). If you drop one of these hints and she doesn't pick up on it, that's it. You can't really say anything else. Just suck it up—it's one day, and remember (we know we keep reminding you), it's *her* one day.

Let's Go Shopping

Before we get into the nitty-gritty here, we're sure you have a million questions about how this usually works. First, assume you'll be the one buying the dress. Don't even ask the bride if she's paying for it. In some cases (very rare, as in she won the lottery and you didn't) she will, but she'll make it clear from the get-go, so you don't need to bring it up. Now brace yourself. If you missed it in chapter 3, here's a refresher: The dress will cost anywhere from $100 to $700. Yikes! Before you say, "Sign me up for the $100 one!" we just want to remind you (again) that it's not up to you; the bride picks out the dress. And to complain about the price is just plain rude. But look on the bright side: Chances are you'll look pretty darn good in that $400 dress—you

won't have to worry about
scratchy fabric or a bad fit.

As far as the logistics go, it
really varies from bride to
bride. Some wedding parties all
go shopping together for the
bridesmaid dress. Other times,
the bride will narrow down the
choices but not pick the exact

dress. She might say it has to be black and cocktail length, or she might
select a specific designer and a certain color and then let you choose the
style (this is a nice way to do it!). Or she could email you a link to her pick
and ask you to go ahead and buy it. Help the bride out here, and if she
tells you the dresses need to be ordered by October 5, don't wait until
October 25. These are the details that will wake her up in the middle of
the night. You don't want to be the bridesmaid who misses the deadline
and has to tape the top of her dress to her cleavage, under her arms, and
across her back because there's so much gaping and you didn't have time
to get the dress altered. Not cute.

Another word of caution here: If you're ordering the dress, make sure you
open up the box a few weeks before your alteration appointment. We've
heard of plenty of stories in which a bridesmaid was inadvertently sent
the wrong dress and didn't realize it until it was too late. It's really easy
to transpose two letters or numbers in a style number, and you could
end up with a strapless floor-length gown instead of the intended halter
neckline, knee-length dress. Colors can be mixed up, too. There may be
fifteen shades of green, and if you end up with the wrong one, it will be
really noticeable—and the bride won't be very happy with you.

another bridesmaid starts constantly bitching to you about the dress

You really want to get rid of negative energy. It's just not good for morale, and considering you're all supposed to be the sole support system on the happiest day of your friend's life, bitterly complaining about her is never helpful. Also, you don't want the bride to catch wind of this kind of talk or accidentally receive a mean text message. You never know what the other bridesmaids might mistakenly do in their fury. So nip the toxic gossiping in the bud ASAP. As soon as you hear or read inklings of a bridesmaid even trying to initiate a big gossip session, say, "It's tough, I know. It's quite a dress. But she is well within her rights to ask us to wear anything she wants. Let's try to think of the positive—at least it's not scuba-diving gear like in the movie *27 Dresses* or an outfit for a hoedown. Wearing this dress for [insert bride's name here] only shows what good, loyal friends we are."

Top 10 Dos and Don'ts of Trying on a Dress

✦ **DO** bring the right undergarments with you. You might think you'll be able to tell how the dress will look when you're not wearing your sports bra from yoga class, but trust us, you can't.

✦ **DON'T** even bother trying on a dress when you're rushed, bloated, or really cranky. Just wait a day or an hour, whatever it takes.

✦ **DO** wear appropriate shoes. You won't necessarily have the exact ones, but at least bring shoes with heels of a similar height. Besides, everything looks better with heels.

✦ **DON'T** assume that if it looks great from the front, it will look great from the back. Look at yourself from every angle.

✦ **DO** unhook, unzip, and adjust everything before you slip the dress on. Sometimes it's difficult to tell if a zipper is all the way down, and you might assume the dress is too tight. Also, if the straps are adjustable, you want to make sure you loosen or tighten them based on how the dress feels on you. Sounds simple, but when you're trying on loads of dresses, it's easy to forget, and you don't want to assume something doesn't fit just because the girl before you wore it differently.

✦ **DON'T** let the flab between your underarm and your boobs make you think you're fat. Everyone has it—even superskinny models.

✦ **DO** move around. You'll be required to walk, dance, and bend at the wedding, so you'd better make sure the dress will let you.

✦ **DON'T** let anyone rush you.

✦ **DO** sit down in your gown. It may look and feel great when you're standing or moving, but it fits completely differently once you take a seat.

✦ **DON'T** insist on ordering a smaller size because you're going to lose weight before the wedding. If you're diligent enough to make that happen, your seamstress can take it in (the opposite is *not* true). A dress isn't a diet program.

She Did It: She Picked a Dress You Don't Like

Take a deep breath. This does happen sometimes, and it can be hard to take—especially knowing that you need to plunk down a whole paycheck for a dress you really don't care for. But keep reminding yourself that this isn't your wedding and it isn't your decision. Basically, you have to suck it up and make the best of the situation. Here are some ideas to make it more bearable.

Ways to Make a Not-So-Flattering Dress Look Better

✦ **THE PROBLEM:** The color washes you out.

THE FIX: Makeup really can help. Use a tinted moisturizer on your body (just be sure to let it dry before you put on your dress). Sweep a little bronzer over your forehead and the top of your cheeks and chin. And experiment with different colors of lipstick.

✦ **THE PROBLEM:** The neckline makes your boobs look enormous—and not in a good way.

THE FIX: Buy a bra that separates your cleavage. When you're wearing one that pushes your breasts together, they look bigger.

✦ **THE PROBLEM:** The hemline hits mid-calf and makes your legs look short and stubby.

THE FIX: Invest in a pair of heels. Just make sure to avoid T-straps or Mary Janes—both of these styles will make your legs look even shorter.

✦ **THE PROBLEM:** You think it makes you look fat.

THE FIX: You'd be amazed at what the right undergarments can do. Invest in a slimmer, and if you're wearing panty hose, get a pair with an extra support panel in the front. Then just add pointed-toe heels. Even if the heels are only an inch and a half, the pointy shape will elongate your legs. Finally, get over it—you don't look fat!

✦ **THE PROBLEM:** It's too sexy.

THE FIX: Will it help if we tell you some bridesmaids would kill for this problem? We're so sorry you're just too sexy. Seriously, here's a perfect opportunity to suggest a pretty wrap, or if it's a winter wedding, let the bride know you think faux fur stoles would be the perfect extra.

✦ **THE PROBLEM:** A big bow is inconveniently placed on the front of the dress—right at the exact spot you want to hide, not highlight.

THE FIX: Find a new attention grabber. Wear a pair of gorgeous chandelier earrings.

✦ **THE PROBLEM:** It's just not my style at all!

THE FIX: Put your personal spin on it by adding accessories that scream "you." Maybe it's a vintage cocktail ring or a pair of killer heels.

What About the Extras?

Like the dress, it's almost always the bridesmaid's responsibility to pay for her own hair and makeup the day of the wedding, as well as her accessories. This includes everything from the shoes to the jewelry to the undergarments. The one exception is that sometimes the bride will give her bridesmaids a piece of jewelry to wear on the wedding day. And it may go without saying, but if she does give you a piece of jewelry, don't show up wearing something else because you're "more of a silver girl."

Beyond the Dress

✦ **LINGERIE:** Depending on the type of dress you're wearing (strapless, with a low back or plunging neckline, etc.), you may need some special support. This is simply not the place to skimp. The wrong undergarments can make even the fanciest dress look unflattering. In addition to the bra, remember the right thong or slimmers and hose—unless the bride has specified bare legs.

get the right bra

Okay, so the dress isn't your standard sheath? No problem! Here's what kind of bra you'll need for any kind of dress.

THE DRESS: STRAPLESS

THE BRA: Strapless, but look for one with silicone "grippers," which will keep it from slipping.

THE DRESS: HALTER

THE BRA: A convertible option. These can be worn three or four different ways since you can take off the straps and reattach them to make a halter, crisscross, or even one-shoulder.

THE DRESS: DEEP V-NECK

THE BRA: Go for a plunge. It sits a little lower and the cups don't have quite as much coverage.

THE DRESS: SCOOP BACK

THE BRA: Skip the bra and use stick-on cups. We know what you're thinking: *Those are for girls with a small chest. This isn't going to work for me.* But, trust us, they come in sizes up to DD.

✦ **SHOES:** Hopefully, the bride will leave the shoe up to you. She may stipulate the color and heel size ("black and nothing lower than two inches"). If you're wearing heels, you may also want to invest in some gel padding or cushioning so your shoes are more comfy. Beware: Spike heels make an outdoor wedding and photo session practically impossible.

✦ **JEWELRY:** Ask the bride if she has any preferences for jewelry: gold, silver, diamonds, or pearls? Big and bold or dainty and demure? If she replies, "Oh, don't worry about it," she's probably planning to surprise her bridesmaids with a gift of matching jewelry. Don't wear

biggest bridesmaid beauty mistakes

"I wore this sexy, glossy, burgundy lipstick to match my bridesmaid dress. . . . It was all over my teeth all night long." —tiggerten

"Green eye shadow. Enough said." —skeller

"I had my first Brazilian wax the morning of, at the hotel spa. Total impulse thing—I thought it would make me feel sexy for the wedding. Wrong. I couldn't sit down; I was in such agony. I had to put a cold pack down my panties just to be able to stand through the hour-long ceremony." —ruthielicious

"I decided I wanted a natural lip, like what Jennifer Aniston had on the cover of *People*. So I bought this nude lipstick. In every wedding picture, I look like a corpse." —illyana91

"I went for a facial the day before the wedding and had a horrible allergic reaction to one of the ingredients in the cream they used. I broke out in an itchy, scaly rash all over my cheeks. I had to take a Benadryl and felt spacey the whole wedding." —saber99

anything so bold that it's distracting. She may want you to reflect your own personal style, but she doesn't want your big "drama piece" to be the focus of the photos. Believe us: Unless she has specifically said otherwise, she's thinking small and subtle earrings and a pendant necklace, not an '80s throwback pair of plastic hoops.

✦ **HAIR:** Going to a pro really does make a difference. Just keep in mind that those group appointments take more time than you think. So get there on time and don't assume there's a big cushion built in; it always disappears somehow. Bring a photo of a model or celebrity—or better yet, of your hair the way you prefer from a previous event. It will save you the discomfort of explaining that ringlet tendrils aren't your style. Also, don't forget to account for touch-ups to your color.

How to Speak "Makeup Artist"

On the big day, when you sit down in the makeup artist's chair, chances are you haven't met the artist before and you don't know her style or tastes—or her skills or talents. You'll have to take it on faith, because she's the one holding the mirror in her back pocket. Here's how to get what you want: Arm yourself with a few pictures of looks you like and know the language.

IF YOU DON'T WANT TO LOOK TOO "DONE UP" OR "FAKE," SAY . . .

"I want to look natural."

OR

"I want my skin to look even but as natural as possible."

KEY WORDS: *Natural, even, everyday self*

IF YOU WANT THE FOCUS TO BE ON YOUR EYES, SAY . . .

"I feel my best feature is my eyes. I want them to pop, and keep everything else neutral."

OR

"I want to play up my eyes."

KEY WORDS: *pop, emphasize*

IF YOU HAVE A FEAR OF OD-ING ON LINER . . .

"I like to keep my eyes very clean."

OR

"I don't wear liner under my eyes."

KEY WORDS: *clean, minimal*

IF YOU DON'T WANT CRAZY-FULL OR TRASHY LIPS . . .

"I don't want to be overdrawn." (Sounds like your checking account, but she'll get it.)

OR

"I want everyday lips."

KEY WORDS: *just gloss, natural lip color*

✦ **MAKEUP:** This is a wedding. The routine you use every morning before work probably isn't enough. Besides, pros are used to doing makeup for the camera, so they have those little tricks that you don't know about to make you look amazing in pictures. Once again, bring photos and explain your preferences early on: Do you like a "big lip" or something more natural? Worried about how much a professional makeup artist is going to cost you? Ask for a touch up rather than a complete application. Or, you can even get an application at a department store—for the price of an eye shadow, you can have your makeup done.

red flags!

Raise your hand if any of these come from the makeup artist's mouth.

"GLITTERY" or "sparkly." This is not a wedding look, unless you're in Las Vegas, and not even then!

"WE'RE GOING TO DO DRAMA." Beware: Makeup will be heavy.

"WE'RE GOING TO DO HEAVY CONTOURING." Contouring is for the red carpet, not for every day (even your friend's "special day").

"LET'S EXPERIMENT!" This is not the day to experiment.

"LET'S DO FAKE LASHES." A lot of brides and bridesmaids ask for lashes, but there are usually tears during wedding ceremonies, and lash glue doesn't always hold.

"YOU'RE GOING TO LOOK LIKE A COMPLETELY DIFFERENT PERSON." Uh, save that for the stage. You should look like yourself, only better.

WHERE TO CLICK?
Take dress matters into your own hands! See the entire collections of top bridesmaid-dress designers in our fashion gallery: TheKnot.com/bridesmaiddressgallery.

CHAPTER FIVE
shower time

throwing a shower for the bride seems simple enough: Invite her friends and family, decorate, and don't forget the food and favors. But there's *so* much more involved: details, decisions, and jobs to delegate. Putting together this all-important prewedding party (along with the bachelorette party, which we'll tackle in the next chapter) can be almost as complicated as planning the wedding itself. And (no pressure here!) as a bridesmaid, it's by far your biggest responsibility. You want the party to be amazing and creative so everyone (including you) has a great time. So take a deep breath and put on your party-planner hat. Even if you've never organized more than a dinner for four, you can do this. We've laid it out for you step by step, with lots of fun and innovative options to get you inspired.

the bride tells you she doesn't want a shower

So she's really low maintenance, shy, busy, cynical, or afraid of placing a burden on you. For whatever reason, she wants a short engagement, a small wedding, and minimal fuss. Say, "That might be how you're feeling now, but what if you look back years from now and wish you'd really reveled in this time and celebrated more? Or at least that you took advantage of having a wedding registry of gifts! I mean, how many times do you get married? Only once! So don't feel bad, because I'm really looking forward to throwing this party. We can keep it simple, I promise. No gold lettering on the invitations or inviting your high school nemesis."

Shower Planning 101

Here's where you're going to need to get proactive. It's up to all bridesmaids and the maid of honor to host this party, so don't assume your role will be to wait for the invitation and show up. The bridal party needs to take the lead here. So get started—these parties take some planning!

Step 1: Pick a Theme

Early on, the bridesmaids should get together and brainstorm about the party. Try to keep the focus on what the bride will like. And remember, the shower isn't just a celebration of her impending nuptials—it's a celebration of *her,* everything that makes her unique, special, and loved. Any time you're stuck on a decision, let the bride's personality be your guide: Is she reserved and traditional, or fun loving and free-spirited? Would she be happy—or horrified—with a video retrospective of her life? And would she want to be in on all the plans, or does she prefer to be surprised? No one knows her better than you, her best friends. So, as you come up with ideas for a theme, consider the happiest moments in her life (her family's annual trip to Cape Cod; the groom's proposal in Paris), and use these times to spark your imagination. The best part about having a theme is that it often makes planning easier and more fun—you can use your imagination to add special touches to the invitations, gifts, food, and entertainment. Stuck on what to do? Here are a few ideas to get you started.

ask carley

Q: Is it okay to ask the bride's mother to pitch in with the cost of the shower?

A: Nope. Sorry, but you can't count on her here. Miss Manners types see it as bad etiquette for the bride's mom to step in and cohost since it could be construed as her trying to get gifts for her daughter. We know what you're thinking: You've been to lots of showers where the mother was the host, right? Most people would say it's fine for the mother to throw the shower, but what's key here is that you don't assume she's going to help. If she wants to be a part of it, she'll let you know. It would make her very uncomfortable if she didn't give you some sort of indication that she wanted to contribute and you just outright asked her.

Top Shower Themes

✦ **CHARITY SHOWER**

WHAT IT IS: Instead of bringing gifts to the bridal shower, guests are asked to bring a donation (food, clothing, or even cash) to benefit the couple's favorite charity.

BEST FOR: The bride who has lived on her own (or with her fiancé) for a while and already has traditional shower gifts (cookware and bath linens) but still deserves a fantastic party. Or a socially responsible bride who's feeling guilty about the whole wedding extravaganza.

PLANNING TIP: Rather than spending cash on favors, continue the theme by making donations to a charity of the bride and groom's choosing.

POTENTIAL PITFALL: There will always be those who feel obligated to buy a gift for the shower. Don't discourage them, but point out that the bride may not use the item if it's something she already owns.

✦ HONEYMOON SHOWER

WHAT IT IS: A travel-themed shower where guests bring gifts that the couple can enjoy on their honeymoon—for day *and* night. Consider going in on a group gift like certificates for massages or gourmet dinners at their honeymoon destination.

BEST FOR: The bride who loves to travel. Or the couple who is paying for the honeymoon themselves (and could use some extra perks).

PLANNING TIP: Play up the couple's chosen honeymoon locale. Use maps of the destination for place mats and serve food indigenous to that region.

POTENTIAL PITFALL: When guests hear "honeymoon shower," some may immediately think of sex toys. Consider calling it a "travel shower" if that seems more appropriate for your crowd.

✦ COUPLE SHOWER

WHAT IT IS: A couple shower is closer to a cocktail or dinner party than it is to a bridal shower. The groom, female and male relatives, and close friends are all invited. The shower can range from an afternoon barbecue to a cocktail party at your favorite restaurant or bar.

BEST FOR: Couples who like to do everything together.

PLANNING TIP: You should still make time for gift opening—hopefully, some guests will bring gadgets the guys will like, too.

POTENTIAL PITFALLS: The guest list will be longer, so costs will go up. Some of the single bridesmaids might feel a little funny if they don't have a date.

✦ GO GREEN SHOWER

WHAT IT IS: A shower that's good for the environment. Consider hosting your soiree in a garden courtyard, and let nature be the main decor.

BEST FOR: The eco-conscious bride who wants to give back with her shower. Or the bride and groom who want to revamp their lifestyle to be more green. Hot registry items: stainless-steel pots and pans, organic-cotton bed and bath linens, and bamboo cooking utensils.

PLANNING TIP: Send email invitations (done by a graphic designer) to save on waste, or use recycled paper and have your invitations printed with soy ink. Give tree saplings or soy candles, or skip favors altogether. Hire a caterer who cooks locally grown ingredients.

POTENTIAL PITFALL: Just because you're going green doesn't mean you have to go granola. Think eco-chic (not crunchy). Ditch the burlap and go with crisp white organic-cotton tablecloths teamed with matching napkins tied with twine. Ask your baker to use organic ingredients, but don't feel the need to go vegan.

✦ BARTENDING SCHOOL SHOWER

WHAT IT IS: A glitzier, nontraditional shower in the evening that's set up more like a classy cocktail party. Hire a local bartender—whether from your favorite bar or from a bartending school—to come and show you how to make some fun cocktails. You can even try out some signature concoctions to serve at the wedding.

BEST FOR: A nontraditional bride who loves a good party! A gift-opening session can definitely occur during the course of the evening, but consider asking guests to bring gifts focused around a theme (like the honeymoon, lingerie, or kitchen gear).

PLANNING TIP: Have an emergency plan B, just in case you're inviting a diverse crowd and the socializing doesn't pick up right away. Try this simple icebreaker: Place boxes of Trivial Pursuit cards around the room and encourage guests to ask each other questions.

POTENTIAL PITFALL: An old-fashioned mother of the bride may not feel comfortable in this swanky setting. Figure out a way to involve her—perhaps she could choose the menu.

✦ POTLUCK SHOWER

WHAT IT IS: Even if they already own the basics, modern brides and grooms can always use a little help in the kitchen. The twist? Everyone gets involved—guests bring favorite dishes (along with the recipe for what they bring) from an assigned cuisine, such as Mexican, Chinese, Thai, or French.

BEST FOR: The bride who loves to cook—and eat! And a smaller group of guests who are eager to pitch in.

PLANNING TIP: Be sure to have a cute recipe box to collect the recipes and give to the bride to get her cookin'. Continue the theme with favors. Think wooden spoons or colorful spatulas tied with matching ribbon.

POTENTIAL PITFALL: Not having enough food. Be superorganized and allow for more food than necessary. If bridesmaid Betty's baked ziti came out a little too baked (aka burnt), you want to have a backup entrée on hand.

✦ DESTINATION SHOWER

WHAT IT IS: First showers moved out of the home and into restaurants and country clubs. Now they're traveling even farther—a weekend at the beach or in Vegas!

BEST FOR: The bride who has some special connection to the destination, like a weekend house she's been going to since she was a kid.

PLANNING TIP: If you're worried about spending a full weekend with all the ladies, plan it around an event, like a private vineyard tour and wine tasting or a spa weekend.

POTENTIAL PITFALLS: The logistics could be a nightmare. For one thing, it's not going to be easy to pinpoint a weekend when everyone can get away. Plus, this kind of destination party will probably be more expensive than a regular shower.

✦ COOKING CLASS SHOWER

WHAT IT IS: A shower can still be a girly gab-fest, but it's even more fun when you learn something. Call in a chef to give a lesson on making quick, delicious appetizers.

BEST FOR: The bride who considers herself a real foodie.

PLANNING TIP: Look around for restaurants that have cooking classes or call stores that sell Viking ranges—some weeknights they open up the showroom for demonstrations and special events.

POTENTIAL PITFALLS:
Oftentimes, only evenings are available. There's a lot of standing for the demos, so if the bride has a lot of older relatives, you'll need to keep that in mind. Consider setting up a few tables and chairs for those who don't watch the whole demonstration.

> *i got creative*
>
> "I organized a shower at a local pottery studio so guests could create hand-painted mementos for the bride." —mocoroco

✦ WINE-TASTING SHOWER

WHAT IT IS: A wine pro will teach the group how to taste. It's especially fun if you tie in the wedding or honeymoon destination. Say the couple is going to Spain; get all Spanish wines from different regions.

BEST FOR: The bride who likes to sip; it's also best with smaller parties.

PLANNING TIP: Assume every bottle holds eight tasting servings, so if you have eight guests and you want to taste four different types of wine, you'll need one bottle of each. After the tasting, figure about half a bottle per person.

POTENTIAL PITFALLS: It requires lots of glasses, so it's best to do it at a restaurant or wine bar. If you do choose to do it in someone's home, have everyone bring glasses (and get ready to wash) or call a rental company. And make sure transport home is available for the more festive guests, if needed.

✦ OUTDOORSY SHOWER

WHAT IT IS: This is a little unconventional. Basically, you kick off with a small party, like brunch at someone's house, open gifts, and then do some outdoorsy activity, like a hike or bike ride.

BEST FOR: The bride who always has her gym bag with her. Nonathletes need not apply.

PLANNING TIP: Make the activity optional for guests. Her grandmother probably doesn't need to hit the trails for a couple of hours.

— DON'T LET THIS BE YOU —

biggest bridesmaid mistake

"We were throwing this huge, fancy shower in a hotel, and we got all the details organized except one thing—we forgot to allow enough time to order the invitations. Turns out it took four to six weeks for the cards we chose to be printed and calligraphed, and we had only two weeks before the RSVP date. We wound up having to handwrite a hundred of them. Nightmare." —leila305

POTENTIAL PITFALL: As with any outdoor activity, you have to watch the weather and be prepared with a rain plan.

Step 2: Pick a Date

A shower can take place three months before the wedding, or it can be the week before. It's all up to you. Depending on where most of the guests live, you may need to schedule it far in advance so everyone can make their travel plans. If most people are local, you'll have more flexibility. Once you've picked a date, set up a planning schedule (see "Your Shower To-Do Time Line" on page 98).

Step 3: Set the Budget

Before any site can be booked or a guest list drafted, you have to know how much money you have to work with. First off, who's paying? Go on the assumption that the whole bridal party will be footing the bill equally. If the maid of honor decides she wants to put in a little more, that's great, but don't count on it when you make your budget. The best way to approach the subject is to email the rest of the bridal party and tell them what you're thinking. Ask for feedback—you don't want anyone to feel bullied into spending more than she thinks is reasonable. If there's a bridesmaid who says she just can't afford to contribute, work something out so she can contribute her effort instead of cash. But whatever you do, don't get the bride involved.

Now you can formulate a budget. Everything that's needed for the shower, from the postage on the invites to the fun party favors, will come out of this set amount. Also, make sure you talk with everyone about her flexibility: If you go over your budget by a few hundred dollars, can you

you can't throw in a few extra dollars if things go over budget

Don't assume this won't happen and everything will be okay. Once you determine how much everyone is contributing, it's okay to say, "So we're all settled on $60 [or whatever amount you come to]? I just want to make sure we've thought of everything because I know I'm not going to be able to give any more than that. Maybe we should forget about the fortune-teller [or insert whatever extra item you could live without] just so we have a little more of a cash buffer."

count on everyone to pitch in more money? You may find that one or two bridesmaids are strapped for cash and can't give more. You then need to decide if one or two of you wants to make up the difference (maybe the maid of honor will) or if you really have a budget that's set in stone.

Step 4: Finalize the Shower Theme

We gave you some ideas for this one already (see page 74). Now you just need to finalize it as a group. Everyone needs to agree on the theme before you proceed. The most democratic way to do this is to just take a vote—and make sure everyone has a say. Also, make sure what you had in mind will still work with the budget you've established.

Step 5: Choose the Place

Planning on holding the shower in a restaurant, private dining room, or other popular venue? You'll probably need to reserve it a few months in advance. You don't have to limit yourself to traditional choices, though. If you're looking for somewhere unique (or if you mess up and plan too late), consider your other options. What about a picnic in a park or at the beach; a backyard clambake; or brunch in an art gallery, garden, or bakery?

20 Questions to Ask Before Booking a Space

1. How much does the place cost? Per hour? Per head?

2. How much decoration will it need?

3. How many people can it hold comfortably?

4. If it's outdoors, where can you hold the shower if it rains?

5. Who's in charge of private events and will be your contact person before and during the party? Tip: Make sure you get his or her name, phone number, and email.

6. How much is the deposit? Tip: You'll probably be asked to give an approximate head count and a deposit (usually 20–50%) up front to hold the date.

7. What's the cancellation policy?

8. If the event runs over, will there be additional costs?

9. Are tips included?

10. What about extra services, like cake-cutting or corking fees?

11. Is the food included in the price?

12. Are there menus to choose from?

13. If it's a restaurant, will the meal be a buffet or sit-down dinner? How many courses are served? Is cake or dessert included?

REALITY CHECK

divide and conquer

You don't want three different bridesmaids calling the same place to see if it's available. Not only is it just plain confusing, but you also may be told the place is booked just because the maid of honor called before to reserve it. Put one bridesmaid in charge of all the location details, so there's a single contact person and no confusion.

14. What type of alcohol is included (wine and beer, top-shelf liquor)? Are you allowed to bring your own?

15. Is there an open bar? For how long? The price?

16. Are you allowed to hire additional entertainment, such as a DJ, band, or photographer?

17. Is audio/visual equipment (such as a DVD player) permitted so you can have a slide show?

18. Are you allowed to come in and decorate the room for the party?

19. Are there any restrictions on what you can and can't do (for example, no hanging things from the ceiling, no additional lighting)?

20. Is there parking nearby? Will anyone be available to help transport the gifts to the car?

Step 6: Create the Guest List

Put one bridesmaid in charge of the guest list and RSVPs. For this, you'll probably want to ask the bride for addresses. You should also check with the bride's mother and future in-laws to find out whether there's anyone they want to include. Just remember that anyone you invite to the shower should be invited to the wedding. The good news: If you're trying to keep the shower intimate, that doesn't mean everyone who's invited to the wedding has to be invited to the shower.

Step 7: Order or Create the Invitations

It's smart to send out a casual save-the-date email or card as soon as you've picked the date. Everyone appreciates the notice. And it's a good way to let your guests know that you and the rest of the bridal party are taking care of it. When it comes to the actual invitations, you can create them yourself, buy a set

that has blanks to fill in, or have them printed professionally. It's best not to go with online invitations unless the shower will be very casual and small or the bride is eco-conscious and prefers as few mailings as possible. Depending on what kind of invitation you get, the fill-in-the-blank type or a simple DIY option is probably the least expensive. Of course, the priciest is to have them custom printed—you'll pay as much as double if you go with this option. If you know the bride is working with a particular designer, it might pay to go with him or her as well.

Anatomy of an Invitation

Not sure what you need to include? We've got you covered. Here's what to say on the invites.

✦ Who the shower is for (we know it sounds obvious, but you'd be surprised how many stories we've heard about people leaving this out!)

✦ When and where it will be held (the time and the exact address of the location, not just the name of the venue)

✦ Where the couple is registered (don't worry, this is *not* tacky)

✦ If it's a theme party, proper gift-giving instructions and dress code (see Etiquette Check

dress code

Here's a quick at-a-glance decoder of what to say when you want guests to dress a certain way.

IF THEY SHOULD WEAR: A COCKTAIL DRESS
SAY: Festive attire

IF THEY SHOULD WEAR: A DRESS OR NICE PANTS AND A TOP
SAY: Casual attire or informal attire

IF THEY SHOULD WEAR: ANYTHING SPORTS-RELATED FOR A SPECIFIC ACTIVITY, LIKE HIKING
SAY: Sneakers and jeans, for example (be specific and tell them exactly what kind of clothes to bring for the activity)

to the left to get an idea of how you word this)

✦ What you need from the guests, such as a recipe card or a memory to share at the shower

✦ If the shower is coed (the bride's great-aunt might want to reconsider giving her that lingerie)

✦ If it's a surprise (just a reminder: We're not fans!)

✦ If there will be a wishing well (see Tradition Tidbit, opposite), and the theme if there is one

✦ The name of the contact, usually the maid of honor, who will handle RSVPs and any questions (the contact should be up for some weird and possibly annoying phone calls, like one the night before the shower from a cousin who wants to see if she should pack a sweater!)

Step 8: Plan the Decor and Favors

The trick here is to make sure the decor matches the mood. And don't just do tabletops. Impress your guests with a grand entrance: fun decorations on doors, even a giant sign announcing the shower and its theme (MELANIE'S HONEYMOON IN VEGAS!). If the prospect of decking out a whole room gives you sweaty palms, just keep these three basic rules in mind.

✦ **CREATE A COLOR PALETTE:** Stick to two colors. They can be pink and orange, blue and brown, or cherry red and pool blue, for example. Having just two shades will make the shower look pulled together.

✦ **TAP INTO THE THEME:** This will help give you ideas and inspiration. If it's an eco-shower, use wheatgrass for the centerpieces; for a cooking class, work with an abundance of wooden spoons.

✦ **PERSONALIZE IT:** Your friend's a fashionista? Decorate with cutouts of gorgeous shoes, fake her photo on a cover of *The Knot* magazine, or serve a cake shaped like a stilleto. No matter her style, use photos of the bride, the couple, her dog, or other meaningful parts of her life. It's these details that make the shower stand out. And, as you know, you might have three, four, even ten showers to go to in any given year. Think of ways to make this one truly unique to the bride.

─── TRADITION TIDBIT ───

wishing wells

Before the time of registries and cappuccino makers, the hostess of the shower brought in some kind of container (it could be a crate or a trunk or even a big box) for all the guests to throw small household items into to start the couple off on their lives together. Many showers these days don't have a wishing well and the gifts are just piled up on a table. If there's a wishing well, use it for smaller, inexpensive items, such as kitchen utensils.

Top 10 Favors

Favors aren't a requirement, but they're a fun way to show off the style of the shower. And, of course, guests like them! Here are a few of our favorites.

1. A donation to the bride's favorite charity

2. A playlist of the bride's favorite tunes and iTunes gift cards

3. Mini jars of homemade preserves (tip: ask the mother of the bride for the bride's grandmother's recipe)

4. Cookies packaged in a little cellophane bag with a cookie cutter attached

5. Pretty teacups or tea infusers and mini tins of loose tea

6. Customized fortune cookies (write your own fortunes on little pieces of paper and slip them into fortune cookies)

7. Potted herbs with a recipe that includes them

8. Monogrammed mini chocolates

9. Travel candles

10. Beeswax candles and a beautiful box of matches

Step 9: Mail the Invitations

Be sure to send out the invitations six weeks before the shower. Ask for RSVPs at least two weeks prior to the date so you have enough time to let the caterer know (or so you know in advance just how much grocery shopping you need to do). Volunteer to be in charge of stuffing envelopes, or better yet, have an invitation get-together and set up an assembly line. Crank up the music and serve some snacks and cocktails. It's a good excuse to hang out with the other bridesmaids and have fun. Just make sure one person is in charge of keeping the list of RSVPs and making last-minute calls to people who haven't responded.

Step 10: Make the Menu

If you're hosting an at-home shower, think about having the party catered: Food can be anything from dim sum to a full-brunch buffet. If you're doing a themed shower, make the food match. Are the bride and groom honeymooning in Venice? Do antipasto and red wine. Don't forget

---

HOT TOPIC

do you have to open the gifts at the shower?

YES: "It's expected, and I think people like to see their gift opened."
—EastCoastBride

NO: "You want to be able to spend time talking and catching up with everyone, not opening gifts. I've been to showers where the bride has spent hours opening gifts, and to be honest, it's boring. Your time is better spent socializing."
—Mknyktas

THE KNOT SAYS: Have the bride open the gifts. Guests really do like to see the bride's reactions, and there's the nosy factor: People want to see what other people bought. There are, of course, some times when opening up gifts just won't work—a destination shower is one of these exceptions.

hors d'oeuvres (everyone loves apps!), be it crudités, cheese and crackers, or pita and a variety of spreads. For dessert, serve cake, pastries, cookies, pie, and/or ice cream, either homemade or supplied from the yummiest bake shop in town. If you're trying to cut costs, it might also be fun to have a potluck shower, asking friends and family to each bring a signature dish or dessert to the party.

If you're having the shower in a banquet hall or restaurant, work with the manager or host to come up with a delicious menu. Keep the bride's tastes in mind as well as any special guest needs, such as vegetarian or kosher dishes.

WHAT TO SAY WHEN

one of the bridesmaids forgets to give you her share for a group gift

This is a toughie if you don't know her very well. Assume it's a mistake and try the gentle nudge. We recommend emailing her a quick message. Here's one that will work: "Hey, wanted to let you know I had the shower gift sent straight to my place, so I'll bring it to the shower. Oh, by the way, my credit card bill just came with the charge on it, so if you could send me the check before the shower, that would be great. You owe me [fill in the blank]. Here's my address." This way, you have another opportunity to remind her at the shower. If you still don't get the money, send a similar email before the bachelorette party asking her to send the money before the party or giving her the option to pay your portion of the bachelorette party bill (thus pawning off the collection issue on the bachelorette party organizer!).

Step 11: Organize the Activities

Every good shower should have three main activities: eating, gift opening, and game playing. One bridesmaid (often the maid of honor) should keep track of which guest gave which present, and another should make sure cards stay with the right boxes (it's a good backup plan in case the list maker misses something). That way, writing thank-you notes won't be a nightmare for the bride. Background music (in keeping with the theme, if it lends itself) can add atmosphere as well. The games can begin right when people start walking through the door and take place throughout the party. You can certainly invent your own. Appoint one bridesmaid to act as the emcee for the games and make sure everyone gets a chance to participate.

a gift-opening assembly line

This is a must (to prevent chaos and a mess!) at the shower. Here's how it works: One bridesmaid should bring the bride a gift to open (and take the already-opened gift to a designated spot); another can dispose of the torn paper; someone can gather ribbons to create the traditional rehearsal bridal bouquet (more on this on page 94); and most important, one bridesmaid needs to jot down who gave what gift (as mentioned on page 91) so the bride doesn't have to rely on her memory when writing thank-yous.

Top 5 Shower Games (Rated by Brides!)

✦ MISSING INGREDIENTS

GREAT FOR: Traditional crowds

HOW TO PLAY: Select ten simple, standard food and drink recipes (examples: brownies, gazpacho, angel food cake, tuna salad, a Manhattan). Type them up, leaving out one ingredient per recipe, and make enough copies for guests to have one of each. At the start of the shower, supply each guest with the recipes, instruct her to write her name on each recipe, and then have her indicate what she thinks the missing ingredient is. While the bride opens her gifts, one of the maids can collect the recipes and tally up points (whoever correctly names the most missing ingredients wins). Award a small, cooking-themed prize, such as a wooden spoon, a pot holder, or an apron.

✦ TWO TRUTHS AND A LIE

GREAT FOR: Breaking the ice

HOW TO PLAY: Each guest must introduce herself and then tell the group three things about herself—two should be true, one should be a lie. The remaining guests must guess which statement was false. When each guest has placed her bet, the "liar" must confess. The truths are often way wackier than the lie, creating opportunities for story swapping (and general hilarity).

3 ways to make the shower more "her"

The more personal the shower, the more memorable it will be. Here are a few ways to infuse the event with fun memories of your friend.

A LIFE IN PICTURES

Everyone must bring a favorite photo of the bride. Put a bulletin board on a table and have people pin up their photos for everyone to see. The high-tech version is of course a digital slide show. If getting the equipment isn't too hard, this is a great bet.

REBECCA: THE MUSICAL!

Get together with the bridal party and write her a tribute—in song. Take a favorite song, find the karaoke version online, and rewrite the words to highlight funny habits of the bride or aspects of the couple's story. Performed by the group, this can be hilarious. (P.S. It pays to rehearse!) Hand out the words to the song so everyone can laugh along.

SIXTY-SECOND STORIES

Ask all attendees to bring a story they can tell about the bride in sixty seconds. Keep things moving by having an actual timer people will push; everyone will laugh—and it makes boring stories brief. Pass around an iPod with a microphone and record it for her to play back later. This also works in video booth form—set up a camera in the corner and let people tell stories for her to watch back at home.

✦ **WEDDING VOWS**

GREAT FOR: Entertaining guests while the bride opens gifts

HOW TO PLAY: Ask everyone to help the bride write the couple's vows, but each person gets to write only one sentence. Circulate two clipboards, one with, "I [bride's name] take you [groom's name] and promise to" and the other with, "I [groom's name] take you [bride's name] and promise to." Instruct the guest to write a phrase under the header, such as: "I promise to . . . not roll my eyes when you yell at sports on TV." The first guest then folds down the first line so that it's hidden and passes the clipboard to the second player. After both his and her versions have made it through the

rehearsal bridal bouquet

Don't let those bows and ribbons from all the gifts go to waste! No matter what kind of bridal shower you have for the bride, it's not at all uncommon for the maid of honor or one of the bridesmaids to collect all of the ribbons and make what's called a "rehearsal bridal bouquet." Historically, this is the bouquet the bride would use at her wedding rehearsal, but even if the bride isn't having any kind of rehearsal, you can still make her one of these bouquets. In fact, nowadays most brides don't even have a bouquet at their rehearsal, but the shower tradition is still carried on. If this is the case, you don't have to get fancy with this bouquet: Just poke a hole through a paper plate to pull long ribbons through as the stem.

group, read the vows aloud for all to hear.

✦ **WEDDING NIGHT PREVIEW**

GREAT FOR: Laughs

HOW TO PLAY: While the guest of honor opens her gifts, a bridesmaid secretly takes note of the bride's exclamations. For example, "Oooohh, it's so beautiful!" or "You'll have to show me how this works, okay?" or "I've always wanted one of these!" When all the gifts have been opened, the mischievous maid will come forward and read the bride's comments to the group as the things she'll be shouting out on her wedding night. We know it sounds corny, but trust us—this party trick is hilarious every time.

✦ **PURSE RAID**

GREAT FOR: Traditional crowds

HOW TO PLAY: This classic shower game requires that every guest bring her purse to the shower (a given). Before the guests arrive, the maid of honor creates a list of objects that are likely to be found in guests' purses. Items can be banal (lipstick, pill box, mints, video-store card) or bawdy (birth control pills, underwear, a condom), but they should start out ordinary and become increasingly more obscure. At the shower, the maid of honor calls out the items on the list, and the first guest to produce

naughty (but nice!) gifts

MAKE-OUT MUSIC

Get personal and burn a CD with sexy songs (starting off with "Let's Get It On") and favorite bedtime tunes.

THE FOOD OF LOVE

Give her a goody basket of bedroom treats: everything from body paints and erotic fortune cookies to an edible bra and panties. Or head to the grocery store and pick up chocolate syrup, honey, or caramel . . . and leave it up to the happy couple to improvise!

LOVE IS IN THE AIR

Consider giving incense, scented candles, or perfume. Tests have shown that the aromas of cucumber and black licorice (for her) and pumpkin pie (for him) are the top aphrodisiac scents. (It sounds random, but that's what the experts say!)

DEEP RUB

Help the newlyweds relax with a couples massage at a spa. Or treat them to an assortment of scented massage creams and oils so they won't have to leave their bedroom. You could also consider giving a guidebook, like *The Art of Sensual Massage*.

REV UP THEIR ROOM

Give them the props to turn their bedroom into a bordello. Silk or satin sheets and piles of velvet pillows ought to do the trick.

---

each object (or the one who has the most, depending on how long your list of objects gets) wins a small prize.

What About the Gift?

Remember that rule about spending 20 percent of your gift budget on the shower present? Keep that in mind when you're shopping—you don't want to blow your budget on the shower and then not be able to get the couple a wedding gift. One way to stretch your

Top 10 Gift Ideas

TRADITIONAL	NEW TWIST
Linen napkins and napkin rings	Gift certificate to a favorite restaurant
Silver picture frame	Digital photo frame
Crystal vase	Flower-of-the-month-club membership
Champagne glasses	Margarita glasses
Bedding	Breakfast-in-bed tray and pj's
Coffeemaker	His and hers travel coffee mugs
China or dessert plates	Sushi and sake set
Lingerie	Bathing suit for the honeymoon
Barware	Case of wine
Luggage	Beach towels and beach bag

money further is to pool it with one or a few of the other bridesmaids. But group gifting can get tricky if you're the one actually buying the gift and you're waiting for the others to pay you back. To avoid having to send uncomfortable emails reminding an almost stranger that she still owes you $35 (or worse, to avoid being out $160 because the four other bridesmaids never paid you for their part of the $200 group gift), always collect the money before going shopping.

If you're not sure what you want to give, you could simply check the bride and groom's registry. They've already gone to the trouble of selecting stuff they really like and want. Seems boring? Well, the bride doesn't think so—she wants you to buy off her registry. Besides, you can always personalize the present by adding something extra. Say she wants muffin tins; go ahead and get them, but then wrap them up with colorful muffin wrappers, a bright baking spatula, and a pretty dish towel. These little extras won't cost much, but they'll make the gift seem special—even if it's just plain old muffin tins. Still stumped? Check out the box on traditional gifts and their modern updates.

Your Shower Job List

If you have a large group, it's a good idea to put a bridesmaid in charge of each task. If you have a small group, divvy up the duties fairly.

RESPONSIBILITY	WHO WILL HANDLE IT
LOCATION	
GUEST LIST	
RSVPS	
DECORATIONS / FLOWERS	
INVITATIONS	
ENTERTAINMENT	
PARTY FAVORS	
SHOWER GIFT	
GAMES AND ACTIVITIES	
GREETERS (DAY OF)	
CLEANUP	

3+ MONTHS BEFORE

- ◼ Talk to the bride about her shower likes/dislikes.

- ◼ Make a to-do list and assign tasks (use our worksheet on page 97).

- ◼ Set the date and reserve the place.

- ◼ Book the caterer.

- ◼ Create the guest list.

2 MONTHS BEFORE

- ◼ Send out save-the-dates.

- ◼ Purchase invitations or the materials you'll need to make them.

- ◼ Finalize menu, decor, favors, music, and activities.

- ◼ Order equipment from a rental company, if necessary.

1 MONTH BEFORE

- ◼ Assemble and address the invitations.

- ◼ Shop for decorations, paper goods, and other party props.

- ◼ Purchase or make favors.

- ◼ If guests have offered to bring desserts and other treats, call to confirm what they intend to bring and adjust your menu.

2+ WEEKS BEFORE

- ◼ Place flower order.

- ◼ Buy your shower gift for the bride.

- ◼ Make a shopping list; buy any hard-to-find ingredients.

- ◼ Purchase liquor if you're having cocktails.

- Pick up any baskets, CDs, cake stands, punch bowls, tea services, or serving platters that friends have offered to lend.

1 WEEK BEFORE

- Confirm reservations.
- Confirm orders and delivery times.
- Confirm RSVPs (call anyone who hasn't responded).
- Assemble and/or wrap favors you purchased.
- Shop. (Save purchasing the perishable foods for the day before.)
- Create a mental floor plan (or even make a sketch) to facilitate decorating and setting up.
- Prepare shower games and activities.

1 DAY BEFORE

- Purchase and prepare any menu items that can be made in advance (or just do prep work).
- Set up equipment, decorations, and favors; set the table(s).
- Touch base with fellow bridesmaids; confirm who's bringing what and ask them to arrive early to help.

THE DAY OF THE SHOWER

- Prepare food or receive deliveries.
- Receive and display flowers (that morning).
- Arrange and set out refreshments.
- Arrive thirty minutes early to address any last-minute details.

 WHERE TO CLICK: We know, you want to research *even more* shower ideas before you decide on the perfect theme. Don't worry, we've got gobs more (and photos) in The Knot shower area: TheKnot.com/showers.

bachelorette, etc.

bachelorette parties are more laid-back and less structured than traditional bridal showers. And, in comparison, they will be much easier to pull together. But you still have to do some planning. There's no "typical" bash, though what usually comes to mind is a group of giggling girls dragging the bride from bar to bar and making her blush in public. You can paint the town red if that's your—or, more important, the bride's—style. But you can celebrate in lots of other ways, like with a nice dinner at someone's house or in a favorite restaurant, a low-key evening at a jazz club, a concert . . . you get the idea. The point is to reminisce, laugh, act goofy, and embarrass the bride at least a little. The bottom line: Whatever you decide to do, just relax and have fun.

Top 10 Bachelorette Party Themes

Over the X-rated bachelorette bash? Here are ten great ideas without a single G-string.

✦ ANTE UP

Some would consider marriage to be a gamble. So why not hold the bachelorette bash at a casino or racetrack? Most have a nice restaurant, and you could also see a show or book rooms overnight. The great thing about gambling parties (other than the free drinks) is that some lucky ladies may walk away with enough money to pay for the bridesmaid dresses, a wedding present, or—even better—another girls' night out! Just remember the odds are against you, so if betting is your thing, put down only what you can afford to lose.

✦ PAMPER PALACE

Suggest a day or weekend spa event and send everyone running for their plush terry robes. You'll forgo junk food and alcohol, but those clean pores and exfoliated elbows will be worth it. Choose a full-service site that offers everything from massages and mud wraps to makeovers and manicures. The bride will appreciate the stress-buster, and you all may find great new looks for the wedding day.

✦ DISCO INFERNO

Who said disco was dead? Why not whisk her off to a hopping nightclub? Whether she's into "Disco Inferno," "Come on Eileen," or something a bit more contemporary, find a place with the perfect special theme night. Dressing up is so much fun!

✦ HEE-HAW

If she's a country girl, the bride might prefer a good old-fashioned Virginia reel. Take her for a night of line dancing at a honky-tonk bar—and don't forget to bring your cowboy boots and hats!

✦ KARAOKE

If you've forgotten the liberating feeling of making utter fools of yourselves, singing loudly off-key in front of a rowdy crowd should jog your memory. There's a reason kamikazes are served in karaoke bars. After all, do you really *want* to remember your performance?

✦ IT'S IN THE STARS (AND THE CARDS)

If the bride knows her sun *and* moon signs plus her fiancé's rising sign, we can predict with almost perfect accuracy that she'll love a New Age party. Hire a tarot-card reader and an astrologer to do everyone's chart. This idea can be a big hit—and not just with the starry-eyed bride. Who doesn't want to know what the future holds? Just steer clear of sticky topics like, oh, compatibility. It would be a bit of a downer for the bride to find out at her bachelorette party that her groom may not really be Mr. Right.

✦ SCAVENGER HUNT

You're adults, but that doesn't mean you have to act the part! A scavenger hunt (complete with clues and a treasure map) will bring out the children in all of you, and prizes can be as grown-up as you like (bottles of champagne or gift certificates for a massage, for instance). Use a friend's house or garden—or even a whole town or city—and be as creative as you dare.

✦ SEND IN THE CLOWNS

A comedy club may seem to be one step up from the Chippendales, but it's a recipe for hilarity, especially when the stand-ups know you're there for a bachelorette party (marriage, sex, and mother-in-law jokes will fly!).

Call the club in advance, and reserve a front-row table. Tell them what you're celebrating, and ask about a group discount if there's a cover charge.

✦ WHERE THE WILD THINGS ARE

Does the bride love the great outdoors? Consider a back-to-nature bachelorette party. Get in touch with your state board of tourism to ask about campsites, and then call locations of interest and ask about rental cabins or tents (if you come up empty, you can rent tents and other supplies at outdoor stores). Also, find out what activities are offered (hiking, canoeing, swimming, fishing, horseback riding). Make sure all guests know what clothes, food, and accessories to pack—and, most important, *remember to bring toilet paper.*

✦ *CERVEZA, POR FAVOR*

Here's a surefire way to make the bride forget all about the wedding-planning madness: Take off for paradise. Depending on the time of year, you can get great off-season package deals on island vacations or cruises.

WHAT TO SAY WHEN

the maid of honor wants the party to get raunchy, but the bride is conservative

In the planning stages, the maid of honor is babbling on about strippers and penis pops and sewing Life Savers candy onto a T-shirt that says, "A dollar for a lick." Speak up quickly before she makes a trip to a party store and spends any money—or gets any more ideas! Say, "Wow, that sounds like it could be a riot, but since this party is for [insert bride's name here], I really think that will make her uncomfortable. Remember how she almost cried when she found your brother's *Playboy* magazine in the recycling pile? I'm not saying this for me—don't get me wrong—but I've been in this situation before, and the poor bride-to-be was just praying for the night to end. I don't want that to happen to [bride-to-be]. She's such a sweetheart, and it's really all about her."

Check with a travel agent about availability and special group rates. If guests are limited by their schedules or worried about finances, look into a trip that doesn't require much travel time or extra expense. With a two-hour flight, you won't waste precious time on a plane when you should be carousing at the tiki bar. If the bride can't fly the coop completely, think about a beach weekend or a few days of skiing at a nearby resort.

she said / she said
NAUGHTY OR NICE?

BRIDESMAID: "We blindfolded the bride and took her to a store where they sell naughty toys, videos, and props. We thought it'd be really fun for her, something she'd never do for herself." —mjznj

BRIDE: "I was mortified. I wanted to die. I wanted to run out of the store screaming." —dcbride95

Bachelorette Party Planning 101

Just because this party is more casual and probably has fewer guests than the shower, don't let that fool you. You still have a lot of work to do to pull it off without a hitch. The biggest question is who hosts it. Virtually anyone can host a bachelorette party. Often the maid of honor and bridesmaids do the honors, but any friend, relative (a cousin, for example), or even coworker can plan this party. If no one has spoken for it and it's down to the month before the wedding, you should get the ball rolling yourself.

TRADITION TIDBIT
equal debauchery for all

Bachelor parties have been a wedding tradition since ancient times, when they gave the groom a chance to "sow his wild oats" before marriage. We're well out of that dark age (thank goodness!), and ever since the 1950s women have been celebrating imminent weddings with their closest pals, too.

The Guest List

All shower guests must be invited to the wedding, but the same isn't necessarily true for bachelorette parties. Chances are that most bachelorette party guests are wedding guests, too, but it's fine to invite coworkers or neighbors who may not be invited to a small or out-of-town wedding. Just check with the bride before you extend any invitations, and be up front about the limited wedding guest list. It's usually best to keep this party pretty small—under twenty, even under ten, is probably ideal.

Decide on a Date

Steer clear of holding these festivities the night before the wedding—the last thing the bride needs is a hangover! She'll be nervous enough; she shouldn't have to worry about getting sick. (The rehearsal dinner is usually scheduled for that night, anyway.) Plan the party at least two or three nights before the big day. Most bachelorette parties take place a couple of weeks before the wedding but after the shower.

Plan Ahead

One person can plan the entire bash, or several people (like the bridesmaids or the clique from college) can collaborate. Some bachelorette hosts ask for a donation from each guest or cohost, depending on the type of party—whether you're renting a private room in a restaurant or taking everyone for an afternoon of spa treatments, for example. Attendees' contributions may range from $50 to $200, but the bride shouldn't have to contribute a dime. Be reasonable and don't go overboard—you certainly don't need to put yourself in debt over this occasion. A fabulous time can be had by all for little money.

Spread the Word
Email or online invitations are your best option—don't even bother with a paper invite.

Gather Tokens of Appreciation
The bachelorette party isn't a gift party in the same way a shower is—presents aren't necessary. That said, this is a great opportunity for guests to give the bride silly gifts, or even sexy ones (like the lingerie that was just too risqué for the shower). It's a good idea for the bridesmaids to inform the guests that bringing a gift is at their own discretion.

Top 5 Must-Have Party Props

Wondering what to bring to the bachelorette bash? Here's what you should put into your bachelorette bag of tricks.

✦ **THE HEADPIECE:** You want everyone you encounter—the limo driver, the mini-mart clerk, bartenders, and cute guys at the bars—to know what's coming when they see your entourage. A small veil is the most popular way to make the bride stand out, but you can also have her wear a glitzy tiara or, better yet, a hilarious wig.

REALITY CHECK

always be prepared

To be extraprepared, reconfirm your designated driver and bring:

✦ a cell phone

✦ extra cash

✦ a subway or bus schedule

✦ the phone number for a car or taxi service

✦ a street map

✦ a list of the bars you'll be visiting, with addresses and phone numbers

✦ **THE DARE-TO-DO LIST:** Create and bring a list of missions for the bride to fulfill throughout the evening. A scavenger-hunt version might require her to score items such as a condom, five men's business cards, a pair of boxer shorts, and other loot. The dares list might include goofy—but not completely humiliating—acts such as serenading an unsuspecting stranger or dancing on a table.

✦ **A BIT OF BURLESQUE:** Add a hint of sass to the bachelorette's outfit to make her feel dangerous, daring, and fabulously embarrassed. A feather boa is perfect. Encourage all guests to bring a naughty accessory or article of clothing for the bride to wear at some point during the evening.

--- HOT TOPIC ---

are strippers a do or a don't?

DO: "I say if the guys can have them, why not the girls?" —valvirgina

"Hell, yeah. That's the best part of any bachelorette party!" —lling23

DON'T: "I think it's tasteless. And humiliating for the bride. I wouldn't want some slimeball sitting on my lap in a G-string." —rhodeislebride

"No. It's nasty!" —tambforever

THE KNOT SAYS: If a stripping male performing pseudo porn sounds silly to you, go for it. (It isn't really meant to be sexy; it's meant to be fun!) If it sounds gross, skip it. We tend to fall on the skip it side—but maybe it's because we'd rather spend our money on mai tais.

scary stripper

When the stripper shows up, he looks like he most definitely has a disease, or the gun on his police officer's uniform looks suspiciously real. Take a minute to assess things before causing a scene. Who is the most sober or discerning person at your party? Does she see the same thing as you, or are you being paranoid? Ask her, and then consult with her about whether you should say something to the bride. She could say, "You're crazy! Let's get the party started!" Or she could be as spooked and grossed-out as you. If so, politely ask him to return with you to the front door, open it, and say, "You know, I think this is probably not our thing. We seem to have misread the bride and what she wants. We will still pay you for your time, but I think you can go home now. Thanks, anyway."

✦ **X-RATED ESSENTIALS:** We know, it's a little immature, but it *is* a bachelorette party. Navigating a jungle full of penis paraphernalia can quickly become overwhelming, so our advice: Make a beeline for the penis sipper and straws. Since the bride is likely to be boozing it up all night, these two items make the most sense, provide a constant laugh, and allow everyone to get in on the phallic fun. (There are usually six straws per pack.)

✦ **DIGITAL CAMERAS:** When the party's over, the energy and excitement of the night will be reduced to a few fuzzy memories, so don't let a single minute of the evening's debauchery go undocumented. Bring at least two cameras. Have the two designated photographers email the pictures or put them up on a photo-sharing site. But before you tag them to her Facebook page, remember, she has employers!

Whether you're mellowing out or whooping it up, here's a checklist for this infamous night. Feel free to adjust the time frames according to your celebration style.

3+ MONTHS BEFORE

- ◼ Ask the bride what she wants (or doesn't want) for the party.
- ◼ Set the date. Shoot for a night three weeks before the wedding.
- ◼ Create the guest list.
- ◼ Going for a destination bachelorette party? Start planning now.

2 MONTHS BEFORE

- ◼ Send out a casual save-the-date email to see if there are any major conflicts among invitees. If you're partying far away, include specifics.
- ◼ Brainstorm possible game plans and party stunts with the maids.
- ◼ If the party will be at a hot spot or out of town, make reservations, order tickets, and figure out lodging and transportation details.
- ◼ Start looking into transportation arrangements.
- ◼ Research and book any talent for the soiree. If you are hiring a stripper, use a company that has an online presence, and make sure you can view a current photo of the performer. Also, don't hire someone who gets paid by the hour; legit strippers charge a flat fee.

1 MONTH BEFORE

- ◼ Send invitations. Emailing and calling are okay, too. Make sure your invitation politely informs guests that a contribution to the festivities will be expected and name the price.

- ■ If you're going with the standard pub crawl, devise the itinerary. Make reservations (even at bars) and ask about bachelorette freebies.

- ■ Make your transportation reservation(s). Do it earlier if you live in a city or are partying during prom season or in the summer.

- ■ If you're partying at someone's home, help the hostess plan. Make a shopping list. Divide to-dos among the bridesmaids: games, decorations, booze buying, iPod and/or karaoke setup.

- ■ Buy fake penis paraphernalia and bachelorette accessories, such as the novelty veil or tiara, candy necklaces, and other naughty props.

1 WEEK BEFORE

- ■ Make a list of the games you want to play with rules and how-tos, lest you forget after too many margaritas. Keep it handy.

- ■ If you're having a scavenger hunt, conspire with your maids and make a list of the mischievous missions the bride will have to fulfill.

- ■ Confirm the venue.

- ■ Confirm RSVPs.

- ■ Confirm transportation arrangements.

- ■ Confirm the entertainment.

1 DAY BEFORE

- ■ Debrief the bride on the basics such as location and guest list.

- ■ Remind guests of the meeting place and time. If there are several stops planned, name the second address for latecomers and give out the cell phone numbers of at least two bridesmaids you know will be on time.

- ■ Reconfirm all reservations.

Other Parties

In case you didn't realize this already, weddings eat up weekend time—and that's not just for the bride and groom. You've probably already noticed this if you've been invited to an engagement party, to go dress shopping, and/or to a bridesmaids' luncheon. Even if things have been quiet on the wedding front for the past few weeks (it was probably a big flurry of events at first), about three months or so before the wedding, those weekend activities pick up again. So clear your calendar, postpone your "it's all about me" time, and gear up for an interesting couple of months.

Even though you're not planning these parties (thankfully!), you'll still be required to fulfill certain roles. As always, you're representing the bride, so pour on the charm and make those guests feel welcome! Here's a look at some of the other parties you'll be invited to.

The Engagement Party

Most likely, the bride's or groom's parents are throwing this party, which usually happens shortly after the happy couple announces they're engaged and includes all those who will be invited to the wedding. In some cases, it may be the first time you actually meet the families and your fellow attendants. It could be a casual pool party in someone's backyard or an all-out extravaganza at a country club. Or it could be a morning brunch or an evening buffet. No matter where or when it is, the couple will go from table to table or group to group (since many are *not* sit-down affairs) greeting family, friends, and probably more than a few people they don't know. Ask the mother of the bride or the bride herself if there's anything you can do to help. Show guests to their tables? Stand at the door and point them in the direction of the bride (or the gift table or bar)? If you see a sourpuss in the bunch or someone who looks lost or uncomfortable, go over and introduce yourself as a member of the bridal party. Not sure how to make small talk? See the box to the right. By all means, have a good time! Eat, drink, be merry, and make sure you help the bride carry all her loot to the car afterward.

FYI, well-wishers may propose toasts at the engagement

CONVERSATION STARTERS
for the parties (and the wedding)

TO SOMEONE STANDING ALONE:
Ask if the person is a friend of the bride or the groom.

TO THE MOTHER OF THE BRIDE:
Tell her how great the bride looks and what a pretty party it is.

TO THE MOTHER OF THE GROOM:
Tell her what a cute couple the bride and groom make.

TO THE GROOMSMAN YOU'RE WALKING WITH:
Share something funny that just happened or you just saw.

TO THE STRANGER SITTING NEXT TO YOU AT THE TABLE:
Share your fondest (not most embarrassing) memories of the bride.

party. The bridesmaids can elect one person to say a few kind words (save the embarrassing stuff for the bachelorette party or rehearsal dinner); usually it's the maid of honor who speaks. Keep it short, sweet, and to the point. If you're not sure if you're supposed to speak—or if it's appropriate—just ask the mother of the bride.

The Engagement Gift

Since you most likely just met the rest of the bridesmaids, you're probably not pooling your funds on a gift. If the bride and groom have already registered, simply choose your gift from what they've picked out. If not, a safe bet is to give something for their home decor: candlesticks, a vase, picture frames, a fresh bouquet of flowers every month for a year, and so on. Save the household appliances for the shower. Keep in mind that engagement party gifts are completely optional (whereas the shower gift really is required, even if you don't make it to the shower itself). Typically, guests spend about the same as they will on the shower gift. If you don't want to feel awkward about arriving empty-handed, a nice bottle of wine or champagne makes a great last-minute gift.

The Wedding Weekend Events

If the wedding is a destination wedding (and sometimes even if it's not), there may be parties or get-togethers the day before the rehearsal dinner. These are usually intimate and pretty casual. The bride and groom might want to go out for dinner or drinks just with the bridal party since the rehearsal dinner will be bigger and includes family and out-of-town guests. Or, there may be some morning activity the day after the rehearsal dinner. This could be an organized outing, such as a hike, day at the beach, or morning at the spa. Typically if the activity is part of the wedding weekend, your wedding invitation will include an insert with all of the details. Look for key words, like "we've set up a golf tournament," or "we've booked out the spa for the morning." These cues will let you know the bride and groom (or whoever's paying for the wedding) are footing the bill.

The Rehearsal Dinner

The rehearsal dinner is a "practice" party traditionally hosted by the groom's parents on the eve of the wedding. A formal rehearsal of the ceremony isn't necessarily mandatory, but most officiants will want to run through the service with the bride, groom, their parents, the wedding party, and any readers (and sometimes musicians), giving everyone their cues for the next day. After the rehearsal, which is usually held at the ceremony site, everyone gathers for a celebratory dinner, where the bride and groom are roasted and toasted. And you—as a member of the wedding party—will most likely be put on the spot as well (in a good way): The bride and groom will thank you for all your help and support and will usually present you with a thank-you gift.

If it's an intimate gathering, everyone may go around the table saying something funny or sentimental about the happy couple. Be prepared! At larger dinners, the maid of honor and best man will be expected to raise a glass.

 WHERE TO CLICK: Need ideas for clubs or other places to do the dirty deed? Find listings of fun bachelorette resources in your local area at TheKnot.com/bachelorette.

CHAPTER SEVEN

this is it: the wedding

it's a day of magic, moments to remember, and, you guessed it, mega stress. No matter how calm, sweet, and considerate the bride has been through all the preparations, she's now undoubtedly a bundle of butterflies. And you can't really blame her. The past year of planning, the loads of money spent, and the prospect of experiencing the most important moment of her life to date are all whirling together in her head—along with "Does this eyeliner look too dark? Are you sure the car is on its way? Where the hell did I put my veil? Who has the wedding bands? Is the photographer getting this shot?" It goes without saying that she has a few things on her mind. First of all, remember that what's even more important than any single task you'll do today is that you remain unfazed by whatever requests are made of you and even the occasional bridal meltdown. Now here's what you should be ready to do.

The 4 Hats You'll Wear

✦ **THE MIND READER:** To ensure she has the wedding she wants, get in tune with the bride. Adjust your antenna if you have to and keep her on your radar: If it looks like she needs to alternate glasses of water with rounds of champagne, put some H_2O in her manicured hand. If you know she hasn't eaten, get her something to chew on. If she gets stuck talking to the groom's great-uncle from Scotland, save her and help her move to another guest. It's all about anticipating her needs and acting on them—even if she doesn't know she has them!

✦ **THE GOPHER:** If the bride has asked you to arrive at her home at the crack of dawn to get dressed, you'll be there with bells on. If she has asked you to hold her huge ball gown skirt with chapel-length train over her head while she goes to the bathroom . . . yup, you'll do it without hesitation. She may ask you to accompany her to the salon the morning of the wedding while she gets her hair and makeup done. She may need you to run some last-minute errands, such as confirming the flower delivery or picking up some out-of-town guests at the airport. Even if it's an imposition, you'll oblige. She can count on you whenever, wherever, whatever.

✦ **THE CHEERLEADER:** A bride can be overcome with emotion—not to mention nerves—when her "I dos" are just a few short hours away. Assure her that everything is perfect and going according to plan. Tell her how beautiful she looks and how amazing this day will be. Give her a hand to hold and a shoulder to lean on. If little problems do pop up, try to run interference so she doesn't freak out.

✦ **THE HAPPY HOSTESS:** At the ceremony and reception, you'll be a warm, charming, approachable representative of the bride. Before the ceremony, you'll be with the bride and her family, helping with little last-minute details, like making sure the bride's dad's boutonniere is on right or wiping that lip print off the bride's cheek (thanks, Mom, for that last-minute kiss—after hair and makeup!). Of course, it will all fly by in a whirl of excitement, emotion, and elation. So don't forget to savor the moments, laugh if little things go wrong (they always do!), take tons of pictures, and tell the bride how happy you are for her. Do your duty, but have fun. Don't forget: In the midst of all the mayhem, it's a party!

The Morning of the Wedding

Hopefully you got a good night's sleep because you need to be on your game today. And, by the way, did we mention that you might also need to be up at the crack of dawn? One of the biggest mistakes bridesmaids make is assuming there's plenty of time. Trust us, the day

---

bridesmaids spill it

"Right before the processional, my friend flipped out and thought she couldn't go through with [the wedding]. I reminded her of all the things she had been afraid of in her life: the SATs, her driver's test, the school play—and how every time she had aced them. It helped her face her fears, and she made it down the aisle . . . phew!" —natdm699

---

will go by much faster than you expect it to. So it really isn't all that crazy if the bride asks you to be at the hair salon at 8 a.m.—even though the wedding isn't until 4 p.m. Don't give yourself only ten minutes to throw on your dress. The clock is ticking! Here are some tips for making the morning go smoothly.

Top 10 Tips for Starting the Day Right

✦ **BE PUNCTUAL:** We know, we're repeating ourselves here, but this one's really, *really* important. You're on a schedule today, and 8 a.m. means 8 a.m., not 8:30 or 8:45. If you're usually "fashionably late," set your clock thirty minutes fast. You might even want to appoint one maid to make wake-up calls.

✦ **EAT SMART:** You're probably not going to stuff yourself silly. In fact, most bridesmaids we know go too far in the other direction—they don't eat because they don't want to look fat in the dress. This isn't smart either. Just stick to lean protein, like a couple of hard-boiled eggs, or fruit and cheese. If the wedding is later in the day or evening, it's smart to have a protein bar or slices of turkey on hand to hold you over. It's also a good idea to bring your toothbrush to use before your makeup application.

✦ **CHECK YOUR LIST:** If you're toting your ensemble, make sure you have all the pieces with you: the gown, the shoes, the stockings, the undies, and the accessories, including bag and jewelry. If there's anything you're bringing for the bride—maybe she wanted you to lend her your diamond studs for "something borrowed"—don't forget them. Put Post-it notes all around your place reminding you—stick one on your bathroom mirror, one next to your keys, and one on your door. You may want to make a checklist the night before, too. The same goes for your makeup if it's DIY. Also, make sure you have your bridesmaid emergency kit (see page 123) handy.

✦ **SET ASIDE TIME FOR THE BRIDE:** Once you're ready, the bride may ask you and the other bridesmaids to assist her with putting on her gown. Make sure you really are ready before you lend a hand. For one, brides often want the photographer there taking pictures and you don't want to be half-dressed in them. It's also not much help if the bride is asking you to button up her dress when your nails are still wet. And here's a warning: Helping the bride get ready isn't as easy as you'd think, so you won't just be sitting around. There are usually miles of fabric, complicated undergarments to cinch up, and tiny hooks or buttons that need fastening. Plus, you want to make sure the bride doesn't smudge her makeup or stain her gown while she's getting into it (a trick that often requires more than one maid's assistance). To ensure that her veil is secure, come prepared with a pack of hairpins.

✦ **PRACTICE BUSTLING:** Make sure you understand how to bustle her train after the ceremony. Most gowns have either a ballroom bustle (it lifts the train up onto the back of the gown and is attached with little buttons or hooks) or a French bustle (it lifts the top layer of the gown under itself and allows for a billowy look; it's fastened with hooks, ties, or buttons). Do a test run in the morning so you're prepared later on.

✦ **DESIGNATE TRAIN DUTY:** Decide who should be in charge of holding and straightening the bride's train as she walks down the aisle and who will smooth it behind her as she stands at the altar. The maid of honor most often handles this.

✦ **NOTE TRADITION:** Do a quick double-check (for tradition's sake): Does she have her something old, something new, something borrowed, something blue?

✦ **BABYSIT THE BOUQUETS:** The maid of honor is often in charge of making sure all the girls get their bouquets and the moms and VIP family members get the correct corsages. Keep a detailed invoice from the florist with you that specifies what colors and types of flowers have been ordered and who will be wearing them. If the boutonnieres are delivered as well, make sure you get them to the groom and his men before the ceremony.

✦ **GET LUCKY:** Many bridesmaids like to give the bride a small good-luck token to carry with her on her wedding day. A few favorites: a shiny penny with the year of the wedding on it, a four-leaf clover, a silver sixpence to tuck in her left shoe (this signifies wealth and good fortune), a small cross or Star of David, an angel charm, a horseshoe charm.

✦ **KNOW WHO'S IN CHARGE:** Make sure you have the name of the maître d', wedding planner, or banquet manager in case something goes wrong during the course of the wedding. If possible, introduce yourself to him or her so that if you need assistance, you're a familiar face.

Hair and Makeup Time Line

On the wedding day, your beauty focus should be on hairstyling and

---

— TRADITION TIDBIT —

a token for the bride

Giving the bride some kind of gift the morning of the wedding isn't uncommon, but don't get stressed out about it. All you need is a little something that's thoughtful. Flowers, a basket of homemade brownies, or a bottle of champagne are all good ideas. But easy does it on the bubbly: You don't want the bride or her party stumbling down the aisle!

makeup. This isn't the time to test out new highlights, schedule a facial, or get a massage. Help set up a schedule with the salon to prevent overcrowding and stick to it!

Beauty Breakdown

The day's primping schedule really depends on when the bride is getting married and how many bridesmaids she has. Fewer girls mean that you can start later; the same goes for an evening wedding. But ideally each girl should have one hour for hair and thirty minutes for makeup. You may decide the best thing to do is to line up several hair and makeup pros so that, say, three or four of you can be getting ready at the same time.

make your own bridesmaid emergency kit

Here's what you should have on hand:

- ✦ Breath mints /spray
- ✦ Cell phone
- ✦ Comb/brush
- ✦ Cash (because you never know)
- ✦ Hair spray
- ✦ Tissues
- ✦ Makeup (for touch-ups)
- ✦ Mirror
- ✦ Nail file
- ✦ Perfume
- ✦ Extra tampons
- ✦ Band-Aids
- ✦ Pain reliever

Aisle Advice

If you've had a rehearsal, you should know who will escort you down the aisle and where you fall in the order of the couples. If not, the officiant will typically give you the rundown (or a refresher course) right before the ceremony so there's no confusion. Usually, there's a long list of

the bride starts to have a meltdown as the processional begins

Perhaps it's the beauty of the music or the moment, but you hear a sniffle behind you. It's the bride. Say, "Are you crying because you're happy? Nervous? Something else? Please don't cry—you'll ruin your beautiful makeup! You look gorgeous, and pretty soon you're going to see the man you love. He can't wait to get a look at you, and you'll feel calm when you see him. Just ignore everyone else in the church; hold on to your dad, and focus on [insert groom's name here]." If all else fails, say, "Would you like me to find your sister or dad, or stop the music? Your mom is already walking down the aisle, but I can go around the side and get her from the front pew—whatever you like."

family members who will file in before you (for who walks in when, see page 127). Make sure to keep your pace slow, smooth, and steady, and keep your shoulders back and down. Take a deep breath before you start walking. Though you'll be tempted, no sprinting allowed! Smile, look straight ahead, and let everyone see how lovely you are. It's best not to spend the entire time you're walking down the aisle looking around for people you know, though it's nice to catch eyes with a couple of people who are familiar. If you look out into a crowd and don't know most of the faces, it can be pretty intimidating. You'll be informed where to sit or stand: usually at the altar, surrounding the bride and groom, or in the front rows. Ignore any guests who make silly faces or obnoxious comments (there are always a few jokers in the pack). If you stumble or trip (you won't be the first bridesmaid to catch her heel in her hem), don't curse, cry, or quit. The show must go on. Smile and keep moving.

When it comes to your coupling, most maids hope for a hunk but often wind up with a less-than-ideal escort. We heard one story about a bridesmaid who got the groom's fraternity brother. "He was a nightmare," she

the ceremony is scheduled to start, but the groom hasn't shown up yet

Do not alert the bride until you have all the facts. Why is he MIA? What, specifically, is holding him up? If he was goofing off with the groomsmen and lost track of time, try to get an estimate of how many minutes he will be delayed. Beginning the service fifteen minutes late won't ruin anyone's day, but it is worth (gently!) notifying the bride.

If it will be thirty minutes or more, talk to the bride and discuss asking the ushers to explain to guests that they might want to go get some air. Give them the options; don't keep them in the dark, because they will get upset sitting and waiting with no explanation. If you tell them, people will be calmer—they understand that they're there to support the bride and groom, and that means acting graciously.

If—God forbid—the groom is late owing to a hesitation and he doesn't know when he'll show up, ask him what he will need in order to make a decision and get there as soon as possible. Gently remind him there are loved ones waiting for him, and it's only considerate and fair to give an answer. If he needs to talk

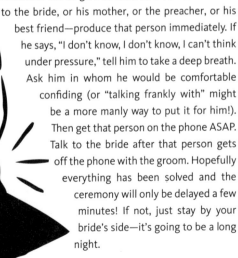

to the bride, or his mother, or the preacher, or his best friend—produce that person immediately. If he says, "I don't know, I don't know, I can't think under pressure," tell him to take a deep breath. Ask him in whom he would be comfortable confiding (or "talking frankly with" might be a more manly way to put it for him!). Then get that person on the phone ASAP. Talk to the bride after that person gets off the phone with the groom. Hopefully everything has been solved and the ceremony will only be delayed a few minutes! If not, just stay by your bride's side—it's going to be a long night.

confessed to us. "He was rude and obnoxious and had a flatulence problem!" Another woman wound up with a married usher—whose wife kept shooting her dirty looks every time she took his arm. And another was paired with a guy about six inches shorter than she was: "His head came right to my cleavage. He was in my boobs all night while we danced." Unfortunately, you have no say in the matter, but it's not like you're marrying the guy; in fact, you'll probably never see him again (unless you go to the couple's anniversary parties). So grin and bear it with grace.

The Ceremony: What to Expect

Some ceremonies are short, sweet, and to the point, while others go on and on and on. So you know what to expect, check out this basic outline of what's usually included in a traditional ceremony.

The Introduction

The music starts; the white carpet or runner is unfurled; all eyes focus on the top of the aisle.

✦ **YOUR ROLE:** Stay out of sight. You should be behind the scenes. Give the bride a quick once-over to make sure she doesn't need any lip gloss or touch-ups.

The Processional

Usually to soft or classical music, the members of the wedding party walk down the aisle to the altar or front rows.

✦ **YOUR ROLE:** Smile and keep your pace so you don't get too close to the person in front of you. For the specific order, see opposite. Once the bride gets into place, take her bouquet if you're the one closest to her.

The Procession Cheat Sheet

The procession is like a flowchart, and it happens a little bit differently depending on the bride and groom's religious and/or cultural backgrounds. Here's the breakdown for two of the most common, Christian and Jewish.

FOR A CHRISTIAN CEREMONY

The officiant, groom, and best man will all be at the altar from the start. Then the procession follows this order:

✦ Groomsmen (they may walk in from the side or accompany the bridesmaids)

✦ Grandmothers of the groom, followed by the grandmothers of the bride

✦ Mother of the groom, followed by the mother of the bride

✦ Bridesmaids (that's you!), starting with the attendant who will stand the farthest away from the altar

✦ Ring bearer and/or flower girl

✦ Honor attendants (this could be anyone from a best friend who couldn't be in the bridal party to a grandparent or godparent who has been given this honor)

✦ Bride, with her escort (usually her father)

FOR A JEWISH CEREMONY

✦ Rabbi and/or cantor

✦ Grandparents of the bride

✦ Grandparents of the groom (they're seated in the first row)

The rest of the procession will stand under the chuppah.

✦ Groomsmen (in pairs)

✦ Best man

✦ Groom, escorted by his parents

✦ Bridesmaids

✦ Honor attendants

✦ Ring bearer and/or flower girl

✦ Bride, escorted by her parents

Prayers and Readings

The officiant may say traditional prayers, and special "honored" guests may read biblical verses, sonnets, or other passages that have significance to the bride and groom.

✦ **YOUR ROLE:** Stand at attention and listen closely. Give any readings the bride asked you to do.

The Vows

The couple may exchange the traditional "With this ring, I thee wed . . ." vows, or they might have written their own personal pledges to each other. The vows are sealed with the placing of rings on each other's fingers.

✦ **YOUR ROLE:** Keep your eyes on the bride and groom. You may be holding the wedding band; if so, hand it over at the right time.

The Pronouncement

The officiant announces the bride and groom are officially Mr. and Mrs. They kiss; the crowd cheers!

✦ **YOUR ROLE:** Breathe a sigh of relief, clap, and wait for the recessional.

The Recessional

Music once again plays and all in the wedding party file out.

✦ **YOUR ROLE:** Follow the bride and groom to the receiving line/cocktail hour or to the allotted place for postceremony photographs.

Top 10 Things to Say in the Receiving Line

Use three or four of these—and mix them up so you're not saying the same thing to three people in a row.

1. "Hello, nice to see you. Welcome" (even if you don't know them . . . and you probably won't).

2. "Congratulations" (if it's a family member of the bride and groom).

3. "What a great ceremony."

4. "The bride looks gorgeous."

5. "I love your dress."

6. "So glad you're here."

7. "You know how to get to the reception, right?"

8. "Isn't this wonderful?"

9. "You couldn't ask for better weather!"

10. "Are you on the groom's side?" or "You look like you must be a cousin."

11 Tips for Looking Great in the Photos

You'll finally know what it feels like to be a celeb—those cameras will be constantly clicking all day and night. It's okay to be a little bit vain. Here's how to make every shot a winner.

1. Assume the camera is always on you. If you're aware you're being watched, you won't be caught off-guard.

2. Make sure everything you want concealed is concealed (like your bra straps, zits, hair roots—you get the picture), and everything you want visible is visible (your sparkling diamond stud earrings, your lovely French manicure, your cleavage!).

3. Freshen up frequently. Apply lipstick and powder throughout the evening so you're not caught looking shiny or glossless on camera.

4. Don't drink too much. You'll look fresher and more natural on film if you're in control.

5. Avoid the temptation to take off your shoes to dance for comfort. You'll look taller and thinner with them on.

6. Keep your chin up when you're in portraits. Looking down can give the appearance of jowls or a double chin. Tilt your head slightly up toward the lens.

7. Don't oversmile. Soft, slightly parted lips are always prettier than flashing all your pearly whites.

8. Know your best side. Check in the mirror before the wedding. Then turn slightly in that direction whenever you're asked to pose.

9. Assume red-carpet position: Angle your body three-quarters toward the camera, one shoulder toward the photographer, one foot in front of the other, and your weight on the back leg. It never fails for celebs!

10. Suck it in. Contract your tummy muscles when you pose and you'll look slimmer in pics, guaranteed.

11. Tense your arms slightly in portraits to give the appearance of more defined upper arms. Try not to hold them flat against your sides—they'll look bigger.

Your Wedding Day To-Dos

Preceremony

+ Fetch anything the bride needs (food, a glass of water, an aspirin) up until the time she walks down the aisle.

+ Track down any members of the wedding party or close friends/family who are running late.

+ Be a witness to the signing of the marriage license.

+ Help set tables with favors or decorate the ceremony or reception site (if it's a small or at-home intimate wedding).

+ Pose for wedding portraits before or after the ceremony.

During and right after the ceremony

+ Hold the rings for the ceremony.

+ Keep track of the bride's purse.

+ Stand in the receiving line with the bride and groom, greeting each guest with a smile and a kiss or handshake.

At the reception

+ Provide the photographer and videographer with some direction on the VIPs in the bride's and groom's lives. Ask the bride or her mom to give you a list of photo must-haves. For example, maybe she wants a shot of elderly Aunt Edythe from Albuquerque or a group shot of her sorority sisters from college.

+ Request songs you know the bride would love to hear.

what do you do with your date?

You're a bridesmaid—which means you're on duty even if you're on a date. It's a tricky situation, and you'll probably benefit from explaining this to your date in advance. Warn him you'll have a lot of responsibilities; you may have to dance with other men in the wedding party and disappear for formal portraits, leaving him to fend for himself for a while. Do your best to spend available time at his side. You'll probably find plenty of opportunities to dance and have fun with your man. And you can always make it up to him later! If he's a friend, don't be surprised if he asks you to be his date at the next wedding he's in!

✦ Introduce people and make sure everyone is having a good time.

✦ Dance, dance, dance. Get those wallflowers out on the floor!

Toward the end of the reception

✦ Make sure the guests who've had a bit too much to drink don't drive home; arrange for carpools or taxis ahead of time, just in case.

✦ Decorate the honeymoon suite for a romantic evening (with rose petals, champagne, votive candles) or the newlyweds' car (with shaving cream, a JUST MARRIED sign, toilet paper) for a silly send-off.

✦ Gather any souvenirs you think the bride might want: napkins or matchbooks with the couple's name on them; the menu from dinner; corks from champagne bottles; the plastic bride-and-groom cake topper. Bring along a small bag or box to store all these mementos.

✦ Collect all of the disposable cameras before guests start leaving. Some mistakenly think they're a take-home favor. Gather them up and then have the photos developed for the bride and groom so they're ready when the newlyweds return from their honeymoon.

Last-Minute Wedding Day Disasters

Every wedding is bound to have a glitch or two. Here's how to head off those headaches before they turn into major messes.

Problem 1: One member of the wedding party is sick and can't make it.

✦ **HOW TO HANDLE IT:** If the party is now unbalanced, rearrange the escorts (one maid can walk down on each arm of one groomsman) or have someone fly solo. If the person missing had a specific job (like reading a scripture), ask the bride if she'd like to have the gap filled by another member of the party or someone else in the bride's or groom's intimate circle, and help her arrange that.

Problem 2: The DJ is a no-show.

✦ **HOW TO HANDLE IT:** Have one or two of the bridesmaids keep the bride calm while another calls to find out where the DJ is. Have an emergency contact list (cell phones as well as office numbers) for all services and vendors. If the DJ's stuck in traffic, get an ETA—and let the banquet manager know what's going on so he or she can extend the cocktail hour if need be. If the guests must enter the reception site to begin the dinner, then wait to have "the first dance" until later in the evening when the tunes arrive. If all else fails, wing it and plug an iPod into the room's sound system!

Problem 3: The wedding is outdoors on a hot day, and a guest says she feels faint.

✦ **HOW TO HANDLE IT:** Don't panic. Ask if anyone is a doctor who can help. In the meantime, get her a glass of cold water or a cool compress for her head or the back of her neck. Get her indoors and in air-conditioning immediately. Ask if there's anywhere she can lie down. Assure the bride that all is well and the guest is being attended to. Make sure someone has a cell phone on her at all times in case of a real emergency.

Problem 4: The florist delivered the wrong color of roses. They were supposed to be pale pink, but they're red instead.

✦ **HOW TO HANDLE IT:** If you can, keep the bride away from the arrangements and get to a phone fast. Call the florist, find out what went wrong, and see if the correct arrangements can be delivered ASAP. If not, here's a fast fix: Have the florist add just a few pale pink roses or at least a pale pink ribbon so they at least reflect the color scheme.

Problem 5: The main course is ice-cold.

✦ **HOW TO HANDLE IT:** Don't let the bride worry her pretty little head about it. Hopefully, guests are polite enough not to complain to her. Hunt down the banquet manager and ask him or her to heat things up. And here's the bright side: Even if the filet mignon was slightly frigid, the wedding cake will surely win raves.

Parts of the Reception

The wedding reception lasts anywhere from two to over four hours and can be anything from a casual backyard buffet to an elegant black-tie affair. It can take place at any time of day. All of the above are the couple's personal preferences, but traditionally, the reception consists of the following.

✦ The cocktail hour. While the bride, groom, wedding party, and families are having formal photographs taken, guests enjoy cocktails and hors d'oeuvres.

- Dinner is served! Guests enter the main reception site. The wedding party is announced: Usually, the groom's parents come first, then the bride's parents, the flower girl and ring bearer, the bridesmaids escorted by the groomsmen, the maid or matron of honor escorted by the best man, and finally the bride and groom.

- The bride and groom share their first dance. The wedding party joins in, and traditional dances may follow (such as the hora), in which all guests participate.

- The first course is served or an announcement is made for people to begin going up to the buffet.

- Special dances (usually in this order): the bride with her father, then the groom with his mother, followed by the wedding party dance (usually with the partner you had at the ceremony).

- The main course is served.

- Toasts are made by the father of the bride, the best man, and/or the maid of honor.

- The bride and groom cut the cake. Cake, coffee, and dessert are served.

- The bouquet and garter are tossed for all single guests (be prepared to jump into this group—no arguments if you're not married or engaged!).

- The bride and groom share a last dance.

- The bride and groom make a grand exit; guests can gather for the send-off (to throw confetti, blow bubbles, wave good-bye, etc.).

- There may be an optional after-party.

A Toast to the Happy Couple

The maid of honor—or a chosen representative of the bridesmaids—might be called upon to say a few words during the course of the wedding. The best man's speech is usually a teasing tale of the groom's misadventures en route to matrimony. You can be funny as well, but you can also be serious or sentimental if that's more your style. If you're panicky about public speaking, then practice, practice, practice. You should plan out what you'll say (don't leave it to the last minute) and have some notes on hand if you're afraid you'll forget under pressure. Here are a few guidelines to a terrific toast.

- Say thank you. Start by expressing how delighted you are to be a member of the wedding party and thank the bride and groom (and even their parents) for allowing you to share this special day with them.

- Make it personal. Share a favorite memory, joke, or anecdote (just nothing too embarrassing!) that will be emotionally significant to everyone.

- Offer encouraging words of advice for their future together. You can choose a quote from a famous personality, a movie, or even the lyrics of a love song. One Knottie referenced *The Wizard of Oz* (since the bride hailed from Kansas): "May you always remember that no matter where life's journey takes you, there's no place like home. And duck if you see a tornado coming!"

+ Wish them happiness, health, and joy in their future.

+ Keep it short and sweet—no more than two to three minutes tops or you'll bore the crowd.

+ Speak slowly, clearly, and loudly.

+ If you're inclined (and have talent), by all means, serenade the pair with a song instead of the standard speech. Or write them an original limerick or poem (just keep it clean!).

+ Speak from the heart. You'll never go wrong this way.

+ Conclude with the standard raising of the glass, saying "To John and Jane," and don't forget to take a sip!

The After-Party

Just when you thought the wedding reception was over, there's the after-party. Even if you're exhausted from all the festivities, you're obligated to make an appearance. There are three types of after-parties: the somewhat spontaneous let's-meet-at-a-bar gathering where guests show up and pay their way;

unique gifts for the bride and groom

You want to give more than just silverware, but how can you find a present as special as the happy couple themselves? Try one of these suggestions, and give one yourself or pool with the rest of the party for a gift the couple will never forget.

ARE THEY DO-GOODERS? Make a donation in their name. You can adopt a tiger and help save endangered wildlife; plant a forest of tropical trees to restore the landscape of Nicaragua; even educate an illiterate child for a year in a developing country.

ARE THEY ARTSY? A framed photo collage spelling out their last name (each photo looks like a letter) would be cool hanging over their bed.

ARE THEY INTELLECTUAL? He's into Hemingway; she's a fan of Faulkner—start their library off with a beautiful first edition of one of their favorite works of literature.

ARE THEY FUN LOVING? Give them a game that's all about them. Lovopoly is like Monopoly, but it has their faces and favorite places on the board!

ARE THEY ADVENTUROUS? Why not give them a thrill they'll never forget, like a sailing trip aboard an America's Cup training vessel, a hang-gliding excursion or hot-air balloon ride, even a chance to drive a real race car around the track?

the our-own-room-in-a-bar route with or without an open tab; and the well-organized-wedding-part-two celebration where guests continue in the open-bar revelry in another room at the hotel with or without added entertainment (a DJ, pool tables, or maybe a sundae bar). Many couples like to keep the party going, even into the wee hours of the morning. So be prepared: If the bride says there are after-hours activities planned, bring a comfy pair of shoes to change into and have a cup of coffee with the wedding cake to keep you awake!

The Postwedding Brunch

So the big night is over and the bride and groom are officially married. If they haven't already left for the honeymoon, the postwedding brunch is their final opportunity to thank their guests and spend a little more time with loved ones. The couple or the groom's parents traditionally foot the bill, and the wedding party attends (unless you're in from out of town and have to catch a flight). It's a casual get-together, usually held at the hotel where guests are staying, a nearby restaurant, or even a friend or relative's home. You can dress casually, and if you were up all night partying, it's okay not to be the first in line at the omelet bar. It's the perfect time to tell the bride what a wonderful wedding it was and how much you enjoyed being her bridesmaid. Be sure to thank her folks, too. Want brownie points? You can ask if there's anything you can do while the newlyweds are on their honeymoon, like collect their mail, take the wedding gown in to the cleaners, or deposit checks in their bank account.

After the Wedding

Did you ever think the day would come when you weren't eating, sleeping, and breathing "wedding"? Well, it's here. The party is officially over. But before you hang up those bridesmaid shoes for good (or at least until the next affair), there are just a few more remaining tasks following the festivities.

✦ Thank the bride's mom and dad (and any other hosts) for a great party. Reassure them that everything was wonderful (even if things didn't exactly go off without a hitch). Tell them how much you enjoyed being a part of it.

✦ Help get the goodies—all those wedding gifts—to the car. Lend a hand to whoever is transporting them home for the bride and groom.

- Congratulate your fellow bridesmaids on a job well done, and promise to stay in touch after the wedding—and mean it.

- Make sure the newlyweds' home and pets are taken care of while they're away on the honeymoon. Offer to walk the dog, feed the cat, water the plants, and so on.

- Send your own thank-you notes. Give one to the bride for choosing you to be such a big part of her day (and, of course, for the gift). And don't forget to send a thank-you to the parents of the bride if they contributed to any expenses for you, such as travel or the dress.

- Prepare the happy couple's place for their return. Stock the fridge with food, fill their home with flowers, and even have a bottle of champagne waiting on ice. And don't forget a huge WELCOME HOME sign on the bedroom door. Or maybe it should say, DO NOT DISTURB . . .

Pamper Yourself!

The last order of business has nothing to do with the bride. Honey, you deserve a break today! You've spent the last several months making sure the bride was well taken care of. Now it's your turn to rest, relax, and blow off some steam.

- Get thee to a spa! Book yourself a mani/pedi and massage, and relax those reception-tired feet.

- Take yourself to a movie and order an extra large bucket of buttered popcorn. Who cares about calories? No more dress fittings!

- Go out dancing or drinking with the girls, and don't mention the "W" word once!

- Treat yourself to a sexy new outfit—one that doesn't require shoes dyed to match!

- Call that cute guy you met at the wedding and ask him out. No worries—you already have two things in common: the bride and groom.

- Let your laundry pile up for a week. Eat cold pizza for breakfast. Stay in your pj's all day. You've taken on so many responsibilities for so long. Finally, you can be silly and sloppy and totally carefree for a day or two.

- Book yourself a vacation. Now that you don't have your duties to derail travel plans, take off for someplace that's exciting and exotic—you deserve a honeymoon, too.

ask carley

Q: Do I have to ask her to be my bridesmaid?

A: When it's time for you to tie the knot, are you obligated to ask the bride to be a member of your wedding party? Well, it would be a nice thing to do, and it's often customary to "reciprocate," but it's not necessarily a must, especially if you're having a small, intimate affair and want to keep the attendants to a minimum. If you're concerned her feelings will be hurt, call her and explain why she's not included. Perhaps she can do a special reading at the ceremony or help plan the shower or bachelorette party (if you're not having any bridesmaids). Most likely, she'll want to help out in some way since you were so helpful to her at her wedding.

CONCLUSION
lessons learned

Who knew this experience could make you a stronger and wiser woman? We did! You've lived through all the chaos and crises, and you now know what it takes to put together a wedding from beginning to end. You've become an expert in party planning, team organizing, and emotional 911. You're well schooled in wedding attire and small talk, and you know where to find X-rated party favors. You've come a long way, baby.

But besides all the technical skills you've garnered, you also understand the thrill of getting married. If this is the first wedding you've been in, maybe you were a little jaded or skeptical before, but now you know how beautiful and emotional a wedding can be. Regardless of how hectic the wedding day became, it was also something you'll remember forever. And of course, you now have that gorgeous dress! (Wink, wink.)

acknowledgments

I want to thank all the people who helped create this book:

TheKnot.com community and bridesmaids everywhere for sharing your stories (even the embarrassing ones), your insight, and your strong opinions.

Sheryl Berk for living, breathing, and reliving all of her bridesmaid days—and remembering exactly what it was like to wear that pink taffeta dress. And thanks to Mary Lynn Blasutta for her clever illustrations.

The Knot team: Rebecca Dolgin, Liza Aelion, Melissa Mariola, Elizabeth Stadele, Ellie Martin Cliffe, Jill Baughman, Amelia Mularz, Tia Albright, and Scott Dvorin for being wedding obsessed and making this book a reality.

My good friend and agent, Chris Tomasino, and the whole team at Potter, especially Aliza Fogelson and Jennifer K. Beal Davis.

My friend Danielle. I was her nightmare of a bridesmaid and it still haunts me. I don't dare share the details here. I can't make it up to you, but I hope this book protects future brides from the same kind of misbehaving bridesmaids.

My family. You make my world go round.

index

B

bachelorette party
  budgeting for, 51
  guests, 106
  invitations, 53
  planning for, 105–7
  strippers at, 108, 109
  to-do time line, 110–111
  top five party props, 107–9
  top ten themes, 102–5
bouquets, 21, 48, 94, 122
bras, 66, 68
bridal gown, 20, 22
bridal shower
  bridesmaids' job list, 97
  bride's resistance to, 74
  budgeting for, 51, 81–82
  children at, 91
  decorations and favors,
    52–53, 86–88
  food and drink, 89–90
  gifts, 15, 51, 89, 90, 92, 95–97
  guest list, 84
  invitations, 53, 84–86, 89
  location for, 82–84
  personalizing, 93
  saving money on, 52–53
  selecting date for, 81
  "surprise" showers, 21
  themes for, 74–81, 82
  to-do time line, 98–99
  top five games for, 92–95
bridesmaid dresses
  alterations, 53
  choice of, 34–35
  complaints about, 64
  cost of, 49, 50
  influencing bride's choice
    of, 58–62
  shopping for, 62–63
  trying on, 64–65
  unflattering, coping with,
    65–67
bridesmaids
  biggest beauty mistakes, 69
  bonding with fellow
    bridesmaids, 30–32
  bridal shower job list, 97
  bringing date to wedding,
    132
  customary expenses, 48–55
  declining invitation to be
    bridesmaid, 16–17, 54
  disagreements among,
    32–35

information "cheat sheets"
  for, 33
male bridesmen, 40–41
with money concerns,
  38, 54
post-wedding day duties,
  139–40
three biggest roles, 11
toasts given by, 136–37
top ten jobs, 12–15
top ten rules of
  communication, 44–45
troublemaker types, 35–41
wedding day duties, 118–20
wedding day emergency
  kit, 123
brunch, postwedding, 139

C

cameras, disposable, 132
children, 91

E

engagement gifts, 114
engagement party, 113–14

F

flowers, 21, 48, 122, 134
food and drink, 89–90, 134

G

gifts
  bridal shower, 15, 51, 89, 90,
    92, 95–97
  engagement gifts, 114
  wedding gifts, 15, 51, 53,
    138, 139
grooms, 21, 125
guests
  annoying, coping with,
    42–43
  at bachelorette party, 106
  at bridal shower, 84
  at wedding, 133–34
  who bring uninvited guests,
    43

H

hairstyling, 49, 52, 69, 122–23
honeymoon suite, 132

I

invitations, 53, 84–86, 86, 89

J

jewelry, 49, 68–69
Jewish ceremonies, 127

L

lingerie, 49, 66, 67–68
lodging, 50, 52

M

maid or matron of honor
  declining invitation to be, 21
  extra efforts by, 22–26
  four biggest roles, 18–19
  toasts given by, 136–37
  top ten jobs, 19–22
makeup, 49, 54, 66, 69, 70–71,
  122–23
marriage license, 21, 131
mother of the bride, 20, 34,
  41–42, 75
music, 133

P

photography, 109, 130, 131, 132

R

receiving line, 129, 131
"rehearsal" bridal bouquet, 94
rehearsal dinner, 48, 115
rings, 21, 131

S

shoes, 49, 66, 68

T

thank-you notes, 140
toasts, 22, 136
travel and accommodations,
  50, 52

W

wedding cake, 22
wedding day
  after-party, 137–38
  bridal meltdowns, 124
  bridesmaid duties, 118–20,
    131–32
  ceremony, 126–28
  groom no-shows, 125
  hair and makeup, 122–23
  last-minute disasters,
    133–34
  processional, 123–27
  reception, 134–37
  top ten tips for, 120–22
wedding gifts, 15, 51, 53, 138,
  139